VISION OF SELF

VISION OF SELF

Written by
Acharya Swami Avdheshanand Giri

Translated by
Dr. Surya Vir Singh, M.Sc., D.Phil

PARTRIDGE
A Penguin Company

Cover Page Designed by Vipin Verma

Partridge books may be ordered through booksellers or by contacting:

Partridge India
Penguin Books India Pvt.Ltd
11, Community Centre, Panchsheel Park, New Delhi 110017
India
www.partridgepublishing.com
Phone: 000.800.10062.62

PREFACE

Acharya Swami Avdheshananda Giriji's writings and orations are brilliant expositions of innate, inborn and natural wisdom (Pragya). His religious austerity and penance while in Himalayas has come to the world in the form of many books in Hindi and spiritual discourses, under the banner of Prabhu Premi Sangh, Ambala Cantt, Haryana, India, of which he is the founder. Shrotryia Brahmnisht Swamiji is a Brahman Gyani of the highest order.

I am one of the blessed disciples of Swami ji to whom he has entrusted the job of translating his works published in Hindi into English for a wider readership with particular reference to those who are keen to get an answer of the question — Who am I?, as well as for those who have the desire to know what spirituality naturally is?

Spirituality Naturally takes you to the understanding of the 'Self' — the Everlasting Eternal Existence, the Truth, the Ultimate Reality (the *Tattva*). It is extremely interesting to know that the source of entire manifestation, living or non-living that we perceive objectively is one and the same.

Vedic principles as enunciated by Rishis and saints in Vedas and Upnishads etc., and the scriptures describing Indian philosophy of spiritual science (science beyond science) very categorically expressed: consciousness is Brahman; I am Brahman, That Thou Am, This *Atman* is Brahman. We all are a part of the same reality. Oneness is the word that suffices the meaning. Once we come to know the 'Self', nothing else remains to know.

For the Vision of 'Self' Swamiji has written on various compositions and facets of spirituality, e.g., *Aatma Aalok, Aatma Avabodh, Aatma Anubhava, Aatma Prateet, Aatma Saurabh* etc, all in Hindi.

The book Vision of Self — presents the deepest insight about the Everlasting Eternal Existence (the Truth, the *Tattva*, the Brahman, the Soul, the Consciousness) and the guidelines for the realization of the same, through various expressions of Acharya Swami Avdheshanand Giri Ji written in Hindi and translated by Dr. Surya Vir Singh a disciple of venerable Swamiji. These chapters were written by revered Swamiji about three decades back during his days of *Sadhana* (spiritual practices) in Himalayas where he spent more than a decade as a recluse.

Acharya Swami Avdheshanand Giri says : 'In the creation it is extremely difficult to be born as humankind. It is the greatest gift of God. As a result of good deeds performed in several earlier births, the ever benovelent God bestow His kindness on '*Jiva*' and grant him this greatest body of humankind for his own salvation and He lives with him in his heart as a hidden knower. Both '*Jiva*' and God live together but are like sunlight and its shadow. '*Jiva*', like shadow has a little light and is not full with knowledge. God is full sunlight and is omnipresent. Whatever knowledge '*Jiva*' possesses belongs to God just as a little light in the shadow belongs to full sunlight'.

Parampujya Gurudev (Acharya Swami Avdhesh*anand* Giri Ji) is an embodiment of peace, purity, happiness, bliss and love. He is a source of light in darkness-Shrotriya Brahmanishth saint of the highest order. Gurudev has spent more than a decade in Himalayas for his '*Sadhana*' (Spiritual endevours) and attained/experienced the highest point of the Truth, the Everlasting Eternal Existence.

Dr. S.V. Singh
Translator and Editor

CONTENTS

Existence

The source of our entire behaviour and attitude is 'I'. The power of sustaining perception or recognition of knowledge derived from personal observation, the impression on the mind not derived from memory, the understanding established by experience and actions and gleaming, is the same 'I'. The entire action, process of thinking and the situation are permeated, encompassed, pervaded, spread through, due to the unit of 'I'. The power of sustaining any manifestation is not possible without 'I'. The manifestation of 'I' in other living creatures is not full, as it is seen in human beings.

What is the meaning of unit 'I'? The complete understanding of 'I' is possible only by dividing the inner-self (*antahkaran*) into its segments. The mind, the intellect, the thoughts, the perception, the resolution, the desire, the object meditated upon and intended, and the ego are actively

1

engaged into actions. The mind is principally active for its likings, the intellect is essentially active for the light of senses corresponding to five organs of the sense and the thought (*Chitta*) is particularly active in pondering upon; and the unit 'I' develops into various forms of conditions and influences. All these together form the inner-self (*antahkaran*).

It is this 'I' that manifests from the inner-self and expands. Among the various shows of powers seen in the entire world, the most important and powerful unit is this 'I'. The unit 'I' is the mother of worldly affairs and behaviour.

What this 'I' is? What is its speciality? Its speciality and actions are identification or unification or sameness. Due to such a speciality and functionality, it can identify or unify with worldly matter and materials, persons, situations, conditions and circumstrances. With whatever or with whom 'I' identifies and unifies, it becomes the same.

As soon as it gets identified or unified with a particular situation or person or matter, it assumes the sameness with respect to the situation or person or matter.

Both known and unknown stay together, sick and healthy, unawareness and awareness, with dormant state, are generally aware in their ownselves but; specifically remain unaware, and as a result of such an unawareness, infatuation, embarrassment, perplexity is manifested. But at the same time, on account of being generally aware, the door for future development and transformation remains open; and therefore one can have the feeling of everlasting existence.

The existence of greater knowledge on the unit 'I' is everlasting and specifically the existence of ignorance is already present, as per the doctrine of absolute unity of the spirit. The birth of specific knowledge is due to the presence of general knowledge. General knowledge is the foundation of absolute knowledge and specific ignorance is the cause of unawareness, resulting in the manifestation of infatuation.

We are not able to live always in one condition. Several variable conditions occur in our lives. Except in the state of absolute unity of the spirit, in all other conditions, such as spiritual ignorance or delusion and profound sleep, knowledge and ignorance both exist together. This rather creates doubts or uncertainty or suspense. Without general knowledge, specific knowledge is supportless and is also devoid of sense of objectivity. In the absence of general knowledge, the specific ignorance cannot be expressed. In the non-existence of the first one, it is not possible to define and ascertain the other one. The most important aspect is that it is impossible to ascertain general knowledge without knowing specific ignorance. General knowledge will remain but it is not possible to define and ascertain the same.

In very distant sky the reflection of milky white brightness of moon, that removes darkness, has also a base. The feeling of non-existence does not exist and there is no question of non-existence of existence (Being). This statement is the firm order.

Truth always exists and it is everlasting. Truth is the foundation of all.

From times immemorial, man is researching on 'Self'. In his continuous journey of research he has analysed, discussed and made commentaries on reducing the distance between own-self and other-self, real and unreal, dull and animate, truth and untruth, matter and energy, self and non-self, selfishness and selfless service, taking vision of 'Self' into consideration. Man has experimented upon in this direction several times in various facets but the result was one and the same. To know about non-existence of the non-existant things, it is necessary to have the knowledge of that thing as well as of its non-existence. The freeness of non-existence alone is not possible, meaning thereby that if the existence of entire visible world is existence, then a witness of such existence is an essentiality and its absence is also, that is 'Existence of Witness'. There is an everlasting 'Witness' of both existence and non-existence. It is the Truth — the *Paramtattva*, by which both existence and non-existance are illuminated. The Truth itself is light that is wisdom or (*Gyan*). The Truth is a free entity is well established and self proven eternity; meaning thereby that only Existence (Being) has the freedom to exist freely and not the non-existence. The Truth is complete or whole in itself. It does not require any other light for its illumination to prove its existence. To define the Truth, it may be necessary to express what the untruth is, but the truth has complete freedom, that is, choicelessness.

The Truth is identical to general knowledge, because in general knowledge, the known, the wisdom and the knower, etc. do not exist. The general knowledge is without attributes. To establish and set this point in the intellect Lord Krishna tells Arjuna—'*Nistrayegunny Bhava*'. The Truth requires some support for unfoldment. For expanse, the Truth needs material idol. Development of expanse requires some shelter and then for formless to form and in form to formless, it is essential to have a support or prop.

The entire visible world or universe, manifestation, expansion, development, extension, amplification, diversity, manifoldness is the play of sense organs and the sense organs are the play of mind. If the play of the power is separated from mind, then mind becomes Soul, like, love and worship. Only Soul remains. In this way the entire world and manifestation are proved to be nothing but one 'Self' or Soul. '*Jo pinde so brahmande*' — the creation of im-positioned world is also imaginary. This thought or imagination is helpful in knowing the Reality of the Universe (essence of the *Tattva*). The imagination is also governed by the 'Witness'. What is available can only be understood by the resources. What is available, how irrelevant it is, can only be known through deeply peerless *Sadhana* or through dense awareness of thought process of highest order. Whatever resource is available to the *Sadhak*, should be utilised to attain the above objective. *Sadhak* should proceed with full faith towards unfoldment of ''Self'. A journey towards 'Self' is the journey to know the Truth.

happiness in defeating the enemy and the never ending rat race for foreign culture and civilization has already tied down the life of man with complexity and confusion. At present, power, fear, untruthfulness and roughness appear to be the perceived realities of human life. Truth, love, non-violence and moral values are shaking and dwindling. By sacrificing his mean ego, one can achieve simplicity. Without simplicity one cannot awake sensations (friendliness, compassion, happiness) in himself. The hills, the vegetations, animals and birds and whatever else is visible all over, in the world and universe cannot be held as subtle. If we are not simple we cannot be sensitive towards the inner messages of nature. The problem connected with halo of lustre, society, the power to rule and *Dharma* are so intermixed that they can be solved only by being simple. Extraordinary intellect and confusion make the problem more complex. In comparison to a confused person, a simple person's observations are more rightful and rational.

A simple person can experience much more rationally and rightfully. The knowledge (*Gyan*) about the reality (the Truth), as stated by many, in the mind of man is so much crowded that the person has made himself unqualified to be simple, rational and sightful experience. To look at these problems a new vision is required and that new vision can be achieved through simplicity. For simplicity a person has to make an inward journey towards 'Self'. When man enters into inward journey, the result is simplicity. The simplicity is not just union with any role model, idol, value and form. Simplicity is innate, naturally blooming virtue, a poetical inspiration. It is also not like that the simplicity is an outward exposition. Simplicity comes out only when the person really withdraws from the greed of worldly material things and diverts himself to understand the reality about 'Self'. Generally a person begins his journey of simplicity outwardly with regard to material things.

The real and the innate simplicity comes out from inside. To become simple is not a problem. The problem is that we want to be simple but we are not sensitive. We can be simple from inside only when we start understanding the numerous obstacles, inhibitions, attachments and desires by which we are bound. We like to remain bounded with various thoughts, propositions and our considerations and values. In the absence of this bondage, the person feels that he is insecure. For the purpose of his security on account of his egotism, he finds himself bounded. From inside we are prisoners but from outside we appear simple. The person is imprisoned in the self-created prison. From inside the person is imprisoned with his own traditions, beliefs and ideals. Simplicity is not possible until we are free or liberated from inside. Therefore, we have to start the journey for simplicity from inside. Whatever is inhere, is out there.

Our society, our living style and our any action, work, are expressions of our external form. Changing our external form without changing inside is not simplicity. Simplicity comes out by itself without making manifestation as a medium.

Therefore, we should begin our journey from inside. Outer manifestation is an indication of our inner state; but to know about our inner state we have to sacrifice and abandon our outer form and behaviour. As our inquisitiveness to find our inner complexities and solutions increases the sensitivity and choicelessness (freedom) comes out.

The mind which is not sensitive, aware and conscious is not worth receiving anything and such a mind is devoid of creative activities. To make one simple by binding with someone may fragment his awareness but not internal simplicity. Outwardly one can resemble simplicity and can exhibit simplicity, but this resemblance is not simplicity. The more one understands the continuous activity of elevation, rising upwards and establishing, the greater are the possibilities of his becoming simple. The greater the inquisitiveness and intensity of understanding 'Self', the simplicity will come out in a similar manner.

The meaning of simplicity can be understood only by a person who is not making any effort to becoming something. Such a mind has an extraordinary receiving capability; for there is no obstruction, no fear, no bondage and no outer compulsion. Thus, such a mind is a natural mind. Whenever a person starts thinking of becoming something and exhibits his potential with a desire to show his achievements, complexities increase and disturb his natural state. Therefore, knowing his actual nature, a person should stay in his natural state. 'To Be is freedom and To Become is bondage'.

By nature we like to be away from complexities, be free from problems and want stillness in fragmented life. It is possible only when we are alert towards 'Self' taking into consideration outward efforts. Any serious practice (*Sadhana*) of thought process, any discovery of beliefs, any effort of practicing righteousness, all come from the same source, which is called *Dharma*. Only a simple person follows *Dharma* in reality. A simple person understands the reality of Soul, that is immortality. It is the need of the present that a person should come out above religion, panth, belief, sect and worldly principles; and recognize the Everlasting Eternal Existence (the *Tattva*). Establishing oneself into truth, love, compassion and friendliness with all, will let us see the entire world as reflection of a single source. Simplicity leads to the perfect absorption of thought into one object of meditation, i.e. Supreme Spirit (*Samadhi*).

DESIRE

The man filled with desire, wish and inclination for victory, vanquishing, triumph, defeating, conquest and splendour, greatness, exalted rank, plenty, power, prosperity, etc is always busy and ever action full. In such an action execution and performance the person's activities grow continuously and the man greatly exhausts his entire energy in these outward efforts. The storms of desire are so fast that sometimes man experiences that these storms have blown him away.

However, the arrangements for security to the problems arising out of these outward storms and chaos are very difficult. In an earthquake the houses collapse, earth cracks, trees fall down, stone rocks split and high altitude hills tear off. In these types of dangerous situations, conditions, sufferings, catastrophies and strong challenges, man is able to survive and secure his existence; but when the gentle shocks of desire-quakes influence the inner self gradually, the entire personality of man and his existence appears to be collapsing and disintegrating. For the *Sadhak* it is necessary to come out of this problem of desire, wish and inclination.

The wish and inclination for power, comfort, immortality, everlasting splendour and magnificence is the truth of desire. What is desire? The desire initiates, compels, and gives birth to inclination and will for instant fulfilment of the many, many desires, and then it is possible for the *Sadhak* to understand the real form of desire. If the *Sadhak* with a mind set for investigation and searching intellect with a *Tattvic* inclination comes to know and penetrates into the root cause of the desire then it is possible for the *Sadhak* to understand the real form of desire. The thoughts full of deliberations of the things that the *Chitta* wants; and the *Chitta* full of desired things is such a chain reaction that slowly drains our energy. Under such conditions we attach ourselves to the things that we want and become one with them. Our entire mental body gets surrounded by desires. Continuous thinking and meditating about material things is much more dangerous than their enjoyment, fruition, consumption and eating.

It is the desire that leads to continuous thinking and meditation of material things. The desire is very sensitive towards fulfilling its aim. Is there any desire which is without sensitivity, objectivity and image? Certainly not. Whenever the *Chitta* gets attracted, there could be either picture or word or thought which provides sensitivity to the *Chitta*. This kind of sensitivity creates great longing, eagerness and attachment towards the desired things. If this sensitivity makes one feel joyful and takes him towards satisfaction, then the *Chitta* wants to achieve that objective image, get attached to it and keep it under his control.

The *Chitta* wants that this pleasure should remain under his control. In accordance with our likings and emotions, the strong waves of desires gradually bond the *Chitta*. When the *Chitta* loses pleasure with one image, one thought, one object, one thing and gets bored, then the *Chitta* gets busy in inventing new sensitivity, new thought, new image and new things. Desires continuously encourage the *Chitta* for new enjoyments, tastes and sensitivities. Rejecting the old pleasures and sensitivities, the mind takes on to invent new items of joy. In this manner desires entice a person for instant acquirement of things. If the *Sadhak* introspects, the process that creates desires, he will find that there is some aim for which the *Chitta* shows greater sensitivity are looked at attentively, then the *Chitta* becomes like an actionless centre. Getting tired with one kind of desire, the *Chitta* wants to fulfil itself with some other desire. The *Chitta* always experiences through sensitivity. Whatever *Sadhana* is performed to attain permanent happiness, is based on some kind of sensitivity. Therefore, the *Chitta* is an instrumental resource of sensitivities.

These sensitivities, howsoever natural they may be, always create unnaturality. Some sensitivities are accidentally creative and are self blooming; but even in these sensitivities, the basic point lies in projection of desire.

If we want to know the origin of desire, then we have to understand the entire process of the poignant hunger of allurements and anxiousness of desire.

Most of the people think that one who has a minimum of accumulation is free of desires. Having only a *kamandal* (a pot) and stick has been taken as indicator for desirelessness. A person who is wearing only loin cloth perhaps may be full of desires, in comparison to the person who is living in a palace. When the *Chitta* of a person is set free, liberated, and released from material things and various attractive situations, then only the person is considered desireless.

Only a person free from greed of getting more and more from taste of words and experiences can proceed forward for constructive work, and with only such a transformation creation of newness is possible. Newness means a state when the reality of things, matter, incidents and situations get revealed. For a person who has lost himself in the woods of desire, it is essential that he cuts down the trees of obstacles in his journey of liberation from worldly desires.

Using the sword of discrimination power (*viveka*) one can know the outcome of the desiers.

Self-thinking in the moments of introspection, self-seeing and intense awareness reveals the reality about desire that can take a person to a higher state of consciousness. In order to enter into the highest state of divine existence, it is essential to be free from desires. Shelter in God, *Sadguru*'s support and intense surrender to one's idol deity can help construct the *Chitta* devoid of desires. The *Sadhak* should persistently meditate upon God with desirelessness and practice continuously his *Sadhana* that leads to renunciation. The *Sadhak* should have full faith in himself and his *Sadguru*. He should believe that he has *Sadguru*'s kindness and God's grace on him. Discarding mean literature, the *Sadhak* should read good literature, on spirituality, morality, humanity and love, etc and step forward with control. Discarding his own weaknesses, vices and negative thinking, he should accumulate virtues and with positive thoughts, practice to direct himself to turn towards 'Self'.

AWARENESS

The main problem of a person is his inability to know what he wants. One spends his whole life in continuously searching the resources to attain his goal and objective. One of the many reasons for the problems of man is lack of fixing his aim and objective. An aimless person is directionless and a directionless person is stricken with discontentment. One should understand what he wants from life. If one can enter into the direction of prayer and meditation, he can understand that ignorance is the reason for all the miseries.

What is meditation? Concentration is not meditation, because it is easy to concentrate well on a thing of liking. Such a person can be cruel and hard hearted as well. It is like the planning of a commandant of army for war and killing. A merchant who wants to earn money can be highly centred on concentration for the purpose of earning money. Concentration means — continuity or permanence of one thought and action. If a person has liking for a particular thing then he can naturally concentrate on that thing; but such a concentration is not meditation. Meditation is to be aware. Truthful awareness is meditation. When there is request, conciliation and asking, how can there be awareness? There is tranquillity and freedom in awareness. To be aware is the source of central part of operation for meditation.

'To be deeply aware', signifies presentation of right importance and values of each thing. The beginning of meditation is self-knowledge, which means to be aware of every step of thought process and motion. It implies to know every layer of one's consciousness, whether good or bad. In order to understand these deep rooted invisible actions, motives, reactions and emotions and to be aware of them; tranquillity in conscious mind is an essentiality; meaning thereby that the conscious mind should be at peace, so that it can understand the hurling and agitation of unconscious mind. The conscious mind remains on the surface and busy in daily activities. It is necessary that this conscious mind should understand appropriately the importance of its activities. It cannot simply create peace and tranquillity through rituals and discipline alone. Peace will be achievable only through unbiased introspection and awareness about our activities.

Prayer means that with great concentration we are listening to the calls of inner-self. The note of musical scale of prayer destroys our inner darkness and creates peace. The tunes of the musical notes of prayer and sound waves create vibrations that help open the door of our inner strength. Prayer purifies emotions of our heart, the thoughts of our mind, determination, imitation of activities. As our awareness expands and thoughts purify, the reality about material things is exposed, that is, their importance can be well understood.

Continuous practice of prayer and meditation creates real awareness in the mind of the *Sadhak* and this real awareness leads the *Sadhak* towards that everlasting *Tattva*, where the Truth of life is hidden. Prayer and meditation should be practiced regularly.

The real wealth of the *Sadhak* is his *Sattavic* strengths. Through meditation and prayer, all the *Sattavic* strengths and infinite strengths hidden in the inner-self of the *Sadhak* get awakened.

DESIRE TO KNOWING THE 'SELF'

Man desires continuous ascent. Man not only possesses the desire to live but contains the natural and original wish to live with dignity. When man gets the support of the collective pervasion (the whole) for entrance into dignified living, he gets filled with a special spiritual enthusiasm. There is no such person who must not have questioned himself — Who am I? What is my original source? What is my past, present and future? What is my destiny? Besides this, the person feels amazement about the mystery of this world and believes in its orderly arrangements. The person is engrossed in the search of reply of such type of conundrum quiz from to find the beginning, out the reality of the material things and the evidence of the Everlasting Eternal Truth, which is fool proof in all stages and times all over the universe. The experience of this mystery is the basic property, present in the source of all human beings.

As long as man does not get the glimpse of God (Brahman), his life is not whole. The one who has lost his direction due to numerous serious catastrophic miseries, cannot achieve liberation by any other remedy but to make an inquiry into 'Self'.'

The unmerciful atmosphere, anarchy, disorders and terror all over the world can be challenged only by the power and strength gained through understanding of 'Self'. The acceptance of oneness of the Soul is the essence of the direct perception of spirituality. Today, it is necessary that man must change his life style drastically. A person is capable of freeing his divine future from misfortune and calamity to the extent to which he is able to change himself. Such a change does not happen automatically. Accepting the high ideals enunciated in spiritual scriptures, putforth by learned persons and the highest order of character of 'Sadguru' (the spiritual master) and change in the usual temperament can bring attitudinal changes. To be aware of 'Self' is responsible for a person's transformation. The gratitude for being 'Self' and the reality about fixity of 'Self' amounts to being submissive and obedient.

When a person with fixity in 'Self', does not work with full awareness, then all the directions come to his help and inspire him towards his aim. The clarity about the purpose of life naturally provides the direction.

In the event of spiritual desires becoming active, the activity to re-discover the awareness takes place; and such an activity makes a person spiritual. Being spiritual means — to abide by *Dharma*. The man desirous of 'Self' realization adores his entire life and this decoration gives birth to a beautiful atmosphere filled with purity. In true sense life of a spiritual person is very simple and straightforward. He is not bonded by the chain of symbols, requests, beliefs, mental emotions and '*Prarabdh Tattva*'. The spiritual person accepts and asserts the reality of the 'Eternal Truth' (Brahman), which is ever present over and above of all *Desh*, *Kaal* and Principles. To be spiritual means, that the person is simple and behaves judiciously in accordance with *Dharma*. A spiritual person is supportive of every nook and cranny — living or non living, to the same degree, as innate of original, splendor and luster of nature do.

The elevated peak of spirituality cannot be touched through those religious beliefs, religious sects, religious rituals and one sided cultures, in which a person smells bondage and indifference for worldly attachments. Only that person can climb to the climax of the peak of spirituality and can achieve the glory of hoisting his flag at the peak, who believes in the weightage of intelligence of the preachers of 'Self', has faith in incessant wisdom of *Tattva* and reverence and veneration in surrendering to the lotus feet of *Brahmnishth Sadguru* (the spiritual master).

The origins of such type of divine arrangements of short rules and ties that have been instrumental in ascent of awareness in human being only since times immemorial, come only from Vedic Dharma (*Sanatan Dharma*).

In the present disarray of arrangements, chaos and societal fragmentation world over, the only guiding instrument available to us is the Vedic Dharma. The human being has drifted and lost his direction and purpose of life that is peace, happiness, love, humanity; which is original 'Self'.

Spirituality provides perceptional knowledge of the same 'Truth', understood by various historical faiths. Spirituality gives strengths to detach from all allurements of this world and next world, which inflame and excite all those weaknesses of human mind, where exist never ending desires, longings of becoming chief, powerful and influential person. The foundation of spirituality is the essence of the values of human being and the start of the importance of his relationship with higher world of reality. Man is able to enter into the kingdom of higher level of consciousness, leaving his animal nature, when he is filled with moral force, control, courage and self-confidence. For the fullest discipline of mind, spirituality contains the key and complete resource to face those hurdles and obstacles and ill—will, which are creating danger to the hopes of existence of a well mannered society, full of beauty, humanity and love.

Spirituality contains that discipline which touches the inner-self, and helps to fight all ill-wills and manners of a person. Man wants that favorable conditions should always remain. Materialistic deceit and imaginations bring uncertainty in life. The man beaten and struck by the strokes of multiple uncertainties takes shelter in those resources which provide him freedom from misfortune. Spirituality is composed from those beautiful arrangements of life, where man can achieve wholeness. The travellers who walk on the path of spirituality experience blissful surprises and astonishments in the root of spirituality.

If the world is in search of wholeness, then all those embodiments have to be left out, which emphasize the materialistic and individualistic side of the person extensively and divide human beings amongst each other. Neglecting the values of *Dharma* oriented and directed development of individual, when we discourage the societal sensitivity towards union with the entire creation, the thought process and behavior of the whole society gets affected. *Dharma* is the wealth of our arrangement. If *Dharma* is reflected as a symbol, as a belief, as a faith to discard and neglect the other principles; undoubtedly it is not a good state of affairs and good sign. Faith, belief and strong traditional attachments have deprived man of the blessings of those divine powers, which are present in his-self.

The spiritual path is faultless, easy to follow and simple. In the spiritual path the beginning of all those possibilities lie, which can make a person get acquainted with the highest order — the Everlasting Eternal Truth — (the *Tattva*). In spirituality there is clash and argument on the purpose of principles and definitions of *Dharma*. All the people come nearer to each other with the support of prayer and meditation of God. Prayer and meditation bring together the divided human community. The hard heartedness of egotism melts down. In worshiping God man feels that the basic foundation of our being one is spirituality.

RIGHTEOUSNESS

The essence of oneness in mankind lies in spirituality. The power, force, capacity and strength to unify the divided and fragmented human communities of different cast and creed having different kind of beliefs, panth, and traditions and segmented nations of this world, rests in spirituality alone. As a result of belief in God, the experiments to establish unity and peace in the entire world failed due to the fact that excessive persistence and sameness was being thrust upon on every person. When the excessive persistence and narrowness of traditions and beliefs, and expansion of community demanded strong support to lead the life in a single style, then in the name of *Dharma* very many unusual phenomenon and calamities occurred, which led to the disintegration of human community, instead of unification. Until and unless the different communities stop thrusting upon their own special formalities and traditions; and recognize the different forms and methods of reaching the same Ultimate Truth through mutual coordination, support and cooperative sense, the peaceful co-existence of human community in an united way will never be complete. *Dharma*, belief, worshipping processes, and rituals are different, but the ultimate aim is the same, that is, to know the Everlasting Eternal Existence (the Truth).

The simplicity is rooted into the reality that provides free and easy support to seekers of the Truth and leads them to the same *Paramatattva*, which can be reflected and abstracted in various ways.

Man is living in such an era where he is highly influenced by resources of comfort. The nature of man had become dependent on machines and instruments; and in the event of relationship becoming mechanical man is compelled to lead a life of slavery. The basic nature of man is faultless and enduring. When man is away from his original nature, he is merciless and miserable. The elements which are ruling the awareness of man, the dangerous environment in which he is living and his nature in the state of discontentment, are all due to excessive attraction and allurement towards physical and material things. Excessive ambitions and the desire for instant fulfillment are giving tortures of hell in the life of man.

Spirituality does not mean to free from attraction but it implies to give adequate importance to the outcome of instant form of attractions. The point of view of a spiritual person towards life and oneness is different from that of a common person. The wealth and eulogy, reality of relationship and devices of a spiritual person are constructed with faultless thoughts, discrimination and patience; whereas a common person is ruled by his demands, traditions, beliefs and carried over notions.

Today in the entire world, under the support of carried — over notions, arrogance and provocative short-lived slogans in the name of *Dharma*, hollow assurances of freedom from calamity are being propagated. This era is an era of extravagance, madness, insanity and excessive passion. Ignoring the well proven *Sanatan* principles, provoking and influencing a community to destroy the basic nature of human being is a worst and vilest crime. It is only the spiritual path that has the force, power and strength to combat the intellectual laziness, idleness and inaction. Spirituality does not mean to be good. The direct meaning of spirituality is to keep an innocent form, enabling to be sensibly cooperative. The purity of spirituality lies in using the worldly things as a medium to tread on the path of righteousness; instead of discarding the worldly resources. Man cannot reach righteous path keeping his eyes closed from elevation.

Spiritual thought process renders the four steps of life, that is — moral, economic, artistic and self development. The message of spirituality is that the righteousness (*Paramtattva*) in the path of life can be achieved, only when one fully understands the reality of physical objects and things in this phenomenal world.

If we understand spirituality in its true sense and follow in a proper manner, then it can bring revolutionary expansive newness, happiness and peace. The wandering man has to understand that the human community is to exist as a unit. Man is not separated from each other like sand particles. Undoubtedly man is bound with a live unit in the form of the body and to making it more expressive and illuminative lies in the ability to support and accept everlasting universal values, which are contained inherently in spirituality. Therefore, if man wants firmly to rise continuously, then he has to spiritually surrender to those who are ever active in establishing the human community, full of hopes, mannerism and spiritual culture, into the Truth of Oneness. Those conditions are love, compassion, kindness and friendliness with one and all in the world. Spirituality is keenly available unhindered for the entire welfare and wellness of human beings. When a man discards his narrow and ignorant beliefs, his existence and follow-up of his entire life gets involved in accepting and supporting the elements which are actively and truly engaged in the welfare of the entire world.

of the presence of death is perishability of entire possessions. Death makes everything useless and meaningless.

In the presence of death all is lifeless. Leaving individualism, the everlasting power of existence of 'Self' and the experience of 'Self' is nectar and pure intelligence (supreme spirit). The existence of 'Self' alone is out of the clutches of death. It is the only *Tattva* that defeats and overthrows death. The joyful victorious death, trembles before the 'Self' (supreme spirit).

The one who compelled death to shiver and tremble was Nachiketa. Nachiketa accepts the life. Understanding the life *Tattva*, and meaning of life and their greatness, he awakes into the 'Self' and stops. Uncovering the mystery of death, Nachiketa becomes whole with the Existence of 'Self'. Everything lies in the jaws of death (*Kaal*), but one who is aware of the mystery of life *Tattva*, that is, 'Self, even when he is in the jaws of death, he becomes above the personification of destructiveness principle. In the span of time or *Kaal*, whatever is there it is perishable and destroyable. Time is the motion of death; time is the wheel of death chariot and time is the wings of death like devil bird. Running and flowing with time is like running and flowing in death. Everyone is running towards the same, and is running in the jaws of death. Think a bit, where are you going? Stop! Look what your entire life is? Have you seen any one's death? Certainly! Did you see any Truth in that death? We are dejected every moment. This process is so slow and sequential that till we do not get acquainted with the Truth of life, it is not revealed. After achieving our wholeness, we are able to know this sequential process. We do not require to open the outer eyes of the body to see this process; but we have to once open the inner eyes to understand the same. The outer eyes of the body show only the death of others, whereas when our inner eyes get opened by subtle thoughts, then to keep ourselves secured for life, strong desire for life is created. When we become aware of the fire, the extinguisher is required to save ourselves.

Knowing the certainty of death, leads to increasing awareness about life. It will enable us to enter into various phases of life and let us know the real meaning and importance of life and consequently generates the courage and sensitivity to greatly respect the gift of God, that is the life as human being.

Running away from life amounts to turning towards death. Therefore, what is going on, observe its reality and accept it. This makes our awareness stronger towards life and understanding the life and its meaning. Death is such a devil-like bird whose claws catch us, as soon as we take birth. Death is such a strong whirlpool in which we have lost direction and can not free ourselves from the wings of that devil like bird. Thoughts are such a powerful tool that even in a whirlpool we can remain calm and quiet and standstill. With the support of productive thought process and deep awareness, it is possible to hold tightly the strings of the horses of death like chariot and go ahead towards life.

In the present age, the entire consciousness of person is going outwards. Looking out there, we are looking ourselves only outside and want to find out the ways and means of our security to escape from death. Having tasted the western philosophy, the desperate intellectual has now collected the courage to divert himself towards ownself. We see the change in the awareness in the world. Investigations are going on all around to find out the Truth of life and Existence. The big powers of the world are busy in eradicating the weaponry. A new beginning has been made to stop the wars. The terribly destructive accidents like chemical wars are being curbed. The scientist who brought death on the earth has now started making concerted efforts for safety and survival of life. The joint consciousness, preservation of the people in the world is taking forward steps towards the Ultimate Truth (the Everlasting *Param Tattva*), safety and survival of life. The collective prayers are being held.

For the survival of human existence and safety, the anxiousness to know life and to give shape to greater possibilities of life, the awareness of the entire world is perplexed and intensely engaged. In the context of this auspicious occasion, it is essential that we should take advantage of this situation and take ourselves towards blissful *Tattva*.

After all, what is the Truth about life? In fact, the life comes outside from inside. In the outer world, there is expansion of the life. Outside is not the centre of the life. In fact the source of the life is the life itself. The centre of the life is man's 'Self'. The natural 'Self is man' own nature and the basic root of its Existence is the energy and the source of life. When a person tries to search the life outside, he neither understands the real meaning of life, nor is he able to enjoy the worldly material things and objects. There are many occasions to miss the opportunities; occasions of self awareness are very rare and thin. There are many occasions, when man gets perplexed, looking for life outside. Thoughts of caring and sharing, benevolence and helping others provide opportunities to go inwards.

Actually the centre of man's life and the centre of expression of Godliness is the same. The entire creation, with the law of succession and development began with the same point of centre and from the same centre concealed development of human personality took place. Before the creation the original *Tattva* existed and the entire creation, as it is today, was in subtle form in the past—like the seed of a tree.

The external features and outer existence of the tree is basically present in the seed in subtle form. Exactly in a similar manner every thing in this creation started taking different forms from the subtlest original *Tattva*. In the creation of this creation, expansion and formation of different objects started taking place. Man also assumed his personality and existence. Consciousness was the first covering of the sequence of creation of man. Subsequently mind, intellect and ego and mental powers started providing material grossness and matter. It is because of material grossness, when man reaches out to search life; he is not able to understand the real meaning of life. Whatever is seen outside, many more times it exists inside. There are very many subtle reasons for the outer gross objective and material world. Similarly behind the existence of man there are very many subtle reasons. Man is ignorant about full knowledge. Whatever he knows is not whole, because all his information is based on out there. Death in a fraction of moment grounds all the information and crashes the ego of the person. A person by removing the outer covering, his extreme existence steps forward towards the centre and he steps towards Soul or God. Stepping forward in this direction is a move towards Everlasting Eternal *Tattva*. In the continuous birth cycle, it is only possible when a person starts the inward journey and practices persistently for a long time. Such an opportunity can be termed as blessed opportunity, when the man looks forward towards 'Self'.

ALERTNESS

In our lives, something is continuously happening. The life is full of action with success and failures; something is being added and something is left out. Actually, what is happening in life? — Challenges, excitements, indexing and some reactions (perpetual challenges and instant reactions). Is this the pace and proceeding of life, or is something else? Existence is entirely different from these aspects.

Existence is not affected by any kind of blow, stroke, wound, misfortune, calamity or their combination, because challenges hit every moment with a new body; but the reactions are old fashioned. Howsoever new the challenge is, the reactions are always old fashioned. When we are alert towards the challenge, the challenge loses its power.

The old imitations and perceptions come from reflections of thought. The perceiver depends on his past. The one, who has to go into thought process in a fresh situation or challenge, meets it with his old experience. Our reactions are based on accumulated experiences. That is why we are not able to judge the new challenge in right perspective. When the residue of the memory vanishes, new experience comes into being and that new experience is absorbed in the 'Self'. It is possible when our traditions, path and the process of imitations are terminated; otherwise the activity of bathing in the Existence remains incomplete. The Existence provides newness and the direction which helps in the journey towards the Truth.

Love is not a remainder. It is neither an experience nor a state. Love is the divine presence of Everlasting Eternal Existence. If one is keen to become aware of this divinity, he has to terminate all his thoughts, agitations, reactions and proceedings of activity.

In the inner world, the challenges strongly react and retard the spiritual brilliance. Therefore, one has to witness the excitements and aggression generated by every challenge with perfect equanimity. The greatest problem is that we do not recognize that challenge at its formative step, despite the fact that we are acquainted with it, and allow it to grow and leave its effect.

In this manner we are continuously getting bonded by excitement – aggression chain. It is not that the excitement-aggression creates duality and disorder; but the mind, with the help of words, images, idols, join us and make us temperamentally a thinker. We start believing that we are the doer. Until and unless words, temperamental reactions and doership vanish, the challenges created by these situations will keep ourselves ignorant from the 'Self'.

The *Sadhak* must experience, how the words excite and create reactions in him. At the time of every excitement, aggression and distraction, it is important to watch the result of the situation with equanimity, ignoring the remainder memory. In this way it is possible to escape the blow of duality. One should always continuously examine this entire process.

The dualism of blow and union are a regular feature of life, remain always active in destroying our existence. To root out this type of activity we should always remain attentive and awake towards our 'Self'. when the thinker is bonded with thought and dualism remain truly vocal, the thinker and the thought creator are different — but the witness is the 'Self'. To be courageously awake about this truth, the entire mysteries will reveal themselves naturally. Existence knocks at the 'Self' and repeatedly enquires — who is the witness of all that is happening. The witness, in his power of 'Self', should also see and hear. The witness can free himself by performing powerful activities in destroying the practice of the thinker possessed with many doubts and getting rid of those coverings of the thinker. It is not necessary to show acceptance by the 'Self' towards the 'Self'. What is necessary is to get awakened towards the 'Self' leaving the other, and awakening the witness in all the reactions. This leads to a splendid and beautiful life. Therefore, one should understand attentively, the path of his thoughts, sensitiveness and their purpose. It is not possible to break the unreal vision, without understanding the inner-self, engrossed with different types of desires, demands and deeds.

It is imperative to be attentive to know every movement of thought and sensitivity, every layer of awareness and deeply hidden reactions inside. Your life must be free from agitation, distraction and conflict. You have to examine meticulously your hardness, cruelty, bondages full of ill-will and your commitments. With the process of such awareness, the process of refinement will start shaking, orderly proceeding will start sprouting and it is the stage when you have to discard, kill and go out; so that you become the observer to witness all the happenings.

You are an observer. You should not hide yourself from this Truth. Thought is a false power, that is, it is a delusion. When thought appears in the form of Truth, thereafter there is no requirement of any thought. The patient attentiveness of awareness, in which we do not have any mental resolve, exposes the 'Self'. Thus, the thought process for the truth ends. In this state, the problem that pinches the heart, the challenges that agitate the existence, get solved easily. When we are aware of Truth, the thought process disappears, meaning thereby the thought, the thinker and flow of thoughts vanish and the musical notes of Existence (Brahman) get exposed by themselves. The Existence (Brahman) with full good will show her radiance, and river of peace, bliss and love start flowing. In the process of such a transformation, the moment observer becomes attentive; the Truth calls/drives you. Exposition of the Truth fills you with Divinity.

Expected attentiveness, awareness, knowledge of thought process and the state of being awake towards the 'Self', creates extraordinary splendor, beauty, and the bliss of Brahman.

WAKEFULNESS

To be attentive towards the 'Self' is wakefulness. Only a wakeful person can proceed towards his goal and aim. To be wakeful means — introspection of the processes going inside, in regard to what is automatically available. In such a state the fountain of spirituality starts springing. Spirituality is not the name for any achievement or experience. It is being vigilant towards the 'Self'. Spirituality is not to escape or to fly away. It simply creates natural watchfulness. When awareness getting attached to the 'Self' starts loving the 'Self' (filled with kindness and affection), you will start identifying the desires. Consequently, the wakefulness will come up and in such wakefulness, the Existence illumines. This self illumination is a kind of spirituality. The illumination does not come from outside. It is also a state of wakefulness, and then the 'Self' gets filled with Existence — force, strength, ability etc.

The power of 'Self' is extraordinary and unparalleled. When the awareness is situated in the pure state of the 'Self', it gets sprinkled with eternal elixir of love. Thus fixing awareness into stillness, in the flow of turmoil of mind and irrelevant thoughts, is the first symptom of wakefulness.

The opportunity of that blissful wetting of a few moments fills the 'Self'. The torturous cages of the hell filled with horror get transformed instantly into heaven.

This will start happening when the awareness starts achieving stillness.

Man is searching outside; all his efforts are outward. He cannot achieve peace without going inward. Hopelessness and illness will remain as such, until one under goes inward journey. At one time or the other, if one person looks inwards even once, he will be astonished with the beauty of 'Self'. It is therefore essential to move towards the 'Self'. The journey towards the 'Self' will totally root out all the conflicts. It is possible when our mind becomes still, calm and quiet. The mind is not to be silenced forcefully. It is not to be concentrated either, using any force. The mind is to be primarily made free from liking-disliking (attachment — detachment), object-matter, place-object of sense, using coordinated wisdom to understand the uselessness of the above mentioned pairs. Subsequently, with deep awareness and determination, the divinity of the Soul and her being separate entity need to be understood. The entire visible world is manifestation, display, expansion, extension development, amplification, elucidation and is meaningless and fruitless, if we do not understand the Everlasting Eternal Existence, the 'Self' (the Truth, the *Tattva*).

Such a thinking and meditation regarding the Everlasting Eternal Existence (the Truth, the *Tattva*), will enable you to keep yourself away from the phenomenal world, despite being a part of it. You cannot forcefully avoid the world. The thing that is removed forcefully comes back repeatedly. Be cautious! The stillness of mind can only be achieved by restraint and proper control. The forceful efforts can only work temporarily, but it may prove to be disastrous.

The things, persons and matters discarded and renunciated forcefully, repeatedly haunt the memory. For example, salt is not taken for a day during fasting but the salt haunts the memory repeatedly (I have not to take salt today . . . .), enviously it is not possible to renunciate only object, thing or person. Everything is perishable, gross, temporary and unreal. Only such a discriminate thinking (what is real and what is unreal), can provide the real knowledge about the thing, object and matter. With this knowledge you will be able to discriminate between real and unreal, worth and worthless, useful and useless, meaningful and meaningless, etc. Normally we waste our energy in doing the work and we remain ignorant about the truth, that is, if cause exists, then appearance of work, accordingly, is but natural. Therefore, we have not to ignore the fact that the work is nothing else but accounts for the cause behind it. Using our wisdom we have to remain extraordinarily alert about the above fact.

It is important that the *Sadhak* remains always awake about the movements of his mind. Spiritual path is not separated from this worldly manifestation and display; but lies in middle of the world. It is true that the environment in which we live has its own effect on us. At such a point we should deeply ponder upon, as to why we are getting influenced. Various attractive materials that provide instant pleasure and create sudden hollowness thereafter do continuously influence us. When they continue to increasingly influence us, we get drenched in their comfort without knowing their reality. Under such a condition, watch your thoughts with concentration. You will come to know about the reality of that allurement and beautiful looking articles. Awareness must be alert towards the Everlasting Eternal Existence, failing which, in the state of unwakefulness (dreaming), it wanders in the world out there, which is full of pleasure of senses. However, it is possible to bring the awareness into stillness, even in wandering state, through wakefulness.

We should know the Truth the Ultimate Reality. We should live a life in the reality. We should embrace the reality. We should acquaint ourselves with the reality to know the 'Self'. How long we will play hide and seek with the reality. One of the main reasons of our miserable and torturous life is, that we live in ignorance about the reality. Living in the reality is innate, inborn and natural.

All additional efforts that we make to be humble, gentle and modest, take us away from the 'Self'. Artificial life and any additional show of extra gentleness, makes us escapist, timid and coward. Non-attachment to sensual objects and immutability makes us courageous, determined and committed. Man performs several kinds of formalities with others regularly, but sometimes he becomes formal with himself as well. By leading the life in a particular style, he deliberately binds himself in a narrow sphere. A person living a mechanical life in a fixed style (food habits, spending time, outfits and environment etc.) is generally ignorant about the 'Self' and this type of ignorance is a kind if dense senselessness. How paradoxical it is that a man is running away from the 'Self'. Stresses and tensions give rise to many kinds of arrogance and agitation. The fleet of stresses and tensions enter into the mind, when the person is living totally on outwardly life. A man who feels sad, hurt, affected and distracted in many ways is unable to understand, why he is full of anguish? And many questions arise in his life.

We are caged in a self-made prison. Our own beliefs and many attachments in life attract towards themselves and we get tied down with many unknown cords.

The inner cords continue to tie us down and we cover ourselves with a new robe, leaving our true 'Self'. This new cover creates fear, laziness, worry, dejection and irritation. They create mental tension and shatter the mental balance. The reality yields freedom from the tensions in life and it is the first step towards 'Self' unfoldment. Mental tension creates several types of aggression and agitation; which give birth to several types of diseases. If we wake-up to know this Truth, we can achieve mental balance and simultaneously our natural state.

Keeping away from natural state, it is seen that man wanders about, in the hope of pleasure and joy based on imagination and memories. He is unable to understand, what he wants? Due to increasingly growing mental pressure and tension, man, often leaving prescribed dutiful thinking, joins prohibitive rule. As if stream of thinking with freedom has disappeared and distractions continue to grow.

In absence of meditation about the Truth, and without recognizing the nature of the 'Self', man appears to be living aimlessly. He looks anxious, distracted, and perplexed. He wants to achieve all at a time. He is filled with the desire of instant achievement. Wandering in the endless woods of increasingly growing desires, he lands into deep distress and unhappiness.

If we recognize, even for once, that spirituality naturally is our need, it is sure that every corner of our existence will become keen to know the Truth and surrender himself to Everlasting Eternal Truth (*Tattva*). Mental balance, control on sensual objects and unknown stream of love of God for us will wake-up all the possibilities to know the 'Self'.

The fact is that, in absence of knowing the 'Self' our entire knowledge is covered with ignorance. We are miserable because we are not conscious about the 'Self'. Ignorance is the cause of all sorrows and sufferings. Awakening towards 'Self' is the first step in the direction of highest knowledge and learning.

RIGHTEOUS PATH

All the knowledge (*Gyan*) born out of sense is relative. Whenever we perceive any object matter through any organ of sense, the knowledge that we get could be considered real with regard to some particular angle and situation. But the same perception may not be considered real with regard to some different angle and situation. Our mental knowledge and intellect is also relative, like knowledge derived from organ of senses. The form in which we perceive the world, that perception is dependent on the specific condition of knower and known, on the special composition and condition of intellect-seizing organs of senses. In case the knower and the known were under different situations and the compositions of the organs of senses were different, then our knowledge about the world and the knower would have been different.

A straight rod placed in a container filled with water appears bent at an angle. With a binocular the distant object appears nearer. With a telescope the small thing appears bigger. In love, even ugliness is dear. For a person suffering with fever, the sweet does not taste sweet. Under these conditions it can be inferred that the entire knowledge is relative. Therefore, it cannot be concluded with certainty that the world we perceive, perse is, the same as we see.

Fortunately, if the sixth sense organ also develops or the five sense organs get eternal divinity, it will be possible that many such powers about which man does not know anything do appear and change the entire stream of knowledge or power of human being.

Therefore, what we perceive is not the real form of the object or matter. Different persons may have similar perceptions of the object; because of the similar grasping power of organs of sense. Therefore, a thing, due to specificity of knowledge and situation, may appear good or bad, ugly or beautiful, small or big, etc. It is also not the real form of the object/ matter. Therefore any perception born out of sense organs cannot be termed as *TattvaGyan* — the knowledge of the Truth. There should not be any difference between reality of the object/ matter and *Tattva*. All the dual perceptions are, therefore, unreal and false. All the differences are just convictions.

The Everlasting Eternal Existence is the Truth, the Ultimate Reality, and that by nature, remains unchanged. There is no modification, no alteration. The highest aim of the life, therefore, should be the real achievement of the Truth (*Tattva*), both internally and externally.

From times immemorial, man, in search of the infinite *Tattva*, is running life after life.

Termination of all the efforts in knowing the Truth (the *Tattva*, the Ultimate Reality) is possible. Talking all the experiences of the world, piercing into the many mysteries of nature which are not piercable, showing the greatness of his intellect through extraordinary inventions, man is running with undisturbed speed. The aim behind this is to achieve happiness. The mystery revealing event, when happened before Rishis and Munis, they spoke the *Param Tattva* is '*Avadmangoachar*' (not describable by mind), because mind and speech are able to deliver relative description, thinking and commitment, and eyes and ears cannot reach there. They could not express their perception and knowledge in words and became silent by saying Neti, Neti . . . . They clearly said that our experience of '*ParamTattva*' is not the issue of preaching, because it is not approachable either by mind, or by eyes, or by speech. Even then they gave a direction towards *Param Tattva*, to understand the importance and greatness of human life with the support of reverential faith. On the strength of that faith, the inquisitive traveler, filled with zeal, is advancing forward. His aim is to know and achieve the Ultimate Reality (*Param Tattva*).

In the midst of experience of duality and worldly affairs and phenomena, to know the presence of that infinite power (*Param Tattva*) and perceptin of non-duality is the aim of life.

Experiencing oneness in manyness is the basic knowledge and that is the aim of life. Whether the knowledge is derived from outer organs of senses or derived from inwards. Wherever our knowledge rests on non-duality in duality, advait in davit, oneness in manyness, it is the experience of recognizing the unparalleled wisdom described in Vedic scriptures. An able scientist by many experiments comes forward to show oneness in manyness.

Now, according to physical science, it is possible to convert energy into matter and vice-versa. Words can be converted into energy and energy can be converted into words. In this way the physical science is also advancing day by day towards Oneness (*Advaitvad*).

PURITY OF THOUGHT

The present age is the age of science and politics. The man of the present age has primarily turned his face away from spirituality. His entire manifestations are related to leading a life of merry-making. If anyone gets inspired towards spintuality by reading spiritual scriptures and keeping company of saints, he likes to invent such resources that are akin to injections in western style of treatment giving instant result; but in spiritual path there is no such solution that allows only a little practice (*Sadhana*). These days a number of such medicines have been invented that temporarily provide forgetfulness about the 'Self'. There are so many intoxicating things available in the market by the use of which man temporarily forgets himself. Some Yogic actions are also being advertised through which concentration of mind on one object is often achieved. There are many centers running in the country and abroad for such Yogic-actions. It is neither so easy to learn Yoga without *Sadhana*, nor is it a thing of business and trading. Yoga needs control and austerity. Even a little control starts revealing results. *Bhava-Samadhi* (State of Being) is a distant thing.

Use of medicines for controlling the organs of senses is like, what has been enunciated in Gita: 'Staying without food or with usage of medicines, the organs of senses become incapable of enjoying their respective objects; but objects of the desires of mind remain active. It is just an external affair. Therefore the resource which can retard the desires is acceptable, and that resource is definitely the control, restraint, austerity and penance'. Spiritual practice is the demand of the present age!

These days there is enormous agitation, conflict, distraction, misconduct, dissatisfaction and terror world over. There is lack of belief, faith and respect in the root that renders peace. In the name of regard and consideration on one hand science is advancing and developing tremendously and on the other, it is losing faith in Existence of 'Self; what a wonder! Scientist is ready to do anything for momentary pleasure and happiness. His vision is fixed on resources of enjoyment. His movements are distracted from '*Sadhya*' (attainable permanent peace and happiness i.e. *Anand*). Wisdom, renunciation and devotion are far off things; the life itself has become a problem for him. The effect of environment is such that all the resources of wisdom, action and devotion are becoming trade and business. As a result he gets fatigue in bliss, unpeaceful in peace, ignorance in wisdom, disease in Yoga and business in *Dharma*. Saints and learned persons are merely miracle producing objects for him. Today we see very rich persons as well as poor ones, but all are miserable. They all are dissatisfied with their state of affairs. Every body is in search of true bliss (permanent happiness).

The persons looking distinguished, educated, disciplined from outside are surprisingly hollow from inside, because of additional artificial civilization. Their situation is pitiable. The root cause of this type of poisonous environment is materialism. Man may believe in God or not, but he must believe in himself. To believe in himself is to believe in God.

How paradoxical it is? The man believes in gross objects and matter identified through organs of sense. His organs of sense are powerless. Therefore, an object better than the desire is useless for him. He cannot use it. The organs of sense are irrational, ignorant, stupid and dull. They are useless without awareness (*Chetna*). The awareness in different organs of sense is the same. Therefore, the true bliss does not lie in organs of sense nor in the material or subtle objects. The true bliss lies in awareness (*Chetna*).

To know this awareness (*Chetna*) is to know the 'Self'. If we are able to do this, we can get the glimpse of *Chetna*. This experience of individual awareness takes us to universal awareness. This is called Yoga. It is called *Karma* (action) and it is called worship. To attain it, we have to practice continuously with full faith. It is not essential to accept virtuous symbols, what is essential is that man must believe in himself. He should believe in some laws and arrangements. At least believe in any symbol and atleast concentrate mind somewhere. It is important to remember that to attain permanent bliss and peace, it is a must to believe in some *Chetan Satta* (conscious power), which is a different *Tattva* from various components of the body. To-day's educated and materialistic class considers collection, accumulation, assemblage, of material things as awareness (*Chetna*). They do not consider awareness (*Chetna*), as a separate entity (*Tattva*). Even if we consider mind, intellect and ego a kind of awareness (*Chetna*), yet we have to believe that they are the manifestations of a separate governing entity (*Tattva*), the Everlasting Eternal Existence. To know mind, intellect and ego is to know God and to know this world. To be free from miseries and worries of this world, it is the only remedy and solution. The light within is Everlasting and Immortal. Our inner Soul is Brahman or Consciousness or *Tattvamase* or *Atma*. She is love, belief and faith. The real bliss is within. The moment this source opens the fountain of bliss starts flowing. The vision changes and the world starts appearing blissful. The objects and the material thing of this world are one and the same, but due to individualistic vision the reaction becomes different. Thus, the bliss or despondency does not exist in the object but in the vision. The change in your vision changes your world. For concentration of mind, thinking and deliberation is an essential aspect. Thinking about past and future cannot help concentrate mind even in three *Kaal*s: because deliberations on the past is meaningless and future is uncertain. Therefore thinking of making the present conditions favourable and happy is useful and productive. To remain always happy is considered to be the virtue of the Soul. In fact it is the blessing and fruit of the *Chitta*.

The root cause of the entire miseries and sorrows of the world is the desire of the organs of sense (*Vasana*, the knowledge desired from memory). The worries derived out of *Vasana* are the cause of being devoid of peace and being miserable. The only remedy is thinking within (introspection). Introspection is the source of energy and power — the source from where the fountain of bliss flows. It is the only resource of restraint and self-control.

Without restraint and self-control a human being is not worthy of being called human being. This human body is gift of God. To understand the Truth, the Everlasting Eternal Existence, this human body is just like a strong boat to cross the worldly ocean. The helmsman, the pilot of the boat is the favourable wind of *Gurukripa* (kindness and compassion of the spiritual master). One who does not use these resources to cross the worldly ocean, is a self-destroyer. These days money and property is being given utmost importance. In the very root of the entire political system, the economic system, it is most prevalent. Today money-worship is the frontline objective of human beings. The imaginations of happiness and sorrow are the product of possession of money and its loss, respectively; but by having money, the pains generated due to shortage of money cannot be overcome. Acquisition of money gives birth to objective desires. Materialistic desires, being relative, have no limits. Fulfillment of one desire gives birth to another. Therefore, the first remedy to get rid of money oriented distress, suffering and agony, is to control the materialistic desires. The true wealth is restraint and control, satisfaction and being unavaricious. The one who is dissatisfied is always in distress and is indigent. One who has no restraint and control on organs of sense is a miser. One who is not dissatisfied is all powerful. The indigent is one who is deeply attached with attractive objects of organs of sense. Self-control and self-introspection generates compassion, endurance, tolerance, forgiveness, kindness and sharing/caring the grief of others; and gradually the distinction between mine and yours vanishes. Beyond human beings, it creates a sense of kindness towards all creatures. The entire world becomes unconditionally lovable. When there is nothing like mine and yours, attachment becomes relevant. The principle of *Vasudhaiv Kutumbkam*: the happiness of everyone is our happiness; the sorrow of everyone is our sorrow — such a feeling is created. Introspection, self-analysis is the gate of heaven and bliss. Thinking about body or body consciousness is the gate of hell — is the cause of deep unpeacefulness. This body is a stack of skin, flesh, muscle/tendon, dualism, marrow and bone. It is filled with filth and dirt and excreta. If a human being is delighted and finds pleasure in such a body then what is the difference between him and an ordinary worm or insect. Repeatedly we have to assemble our thoughts in the above mentioned manner and unite ourselves with them. First we should give up the desires generated out of our own will and mental resolve. No mental resolve for wishes, will and desires (*Vasana*). Slowly and slowly restrain your organs of sense and try to understand the trading-business of organism of sense run by your attitude. Thereafter very carefully go within. Mind is very tremulous, it runs towards outer objects. It is to be focused at some centre. Slowly and slowly mind is to be diverted towards self-analysis and introspection. In this manner real and natural source will get awakened. The entire manifestation will appear under the governance of one source, the Everlasting Eternal Existence, the *Tattva*, the Truth, the consciousness, the Brahman, whatever we may call. The original awareness (*Chetna*) is from the *Tattva*. The sure shot of medicine for the mental diseases of man are introspection, 'Self' unfoldment and unconditional love. The feeling of unconditional love automatically results in journey within and the journey towards the 'Self' awakens unconditional love and unconditional love is a very simple and practical process, which is beyond *Desh*, *Kaal*, *Dharma*, *Sampradaya*, caste creed and group, country, time and organization.

A human being belonging to any country, caste, creed, group can adopt this technique for his peace and happiness. Once the technique is mastered, there is bliss and bliss and nothing else. It is called to know the 'Self'. It is also termed perception of *Para-Brahman.* One who has attained realization of love in the bliss, for him the entire world is delighting, pleasing, gladdening. All the trees are the trees of heaven. The entire water is *Ganga Jal.* All activities are pure. All the languages are the voice of Veda. The entire earth is Kashi (the land of Shiv). All the efforts are for the welfare of others. Therefore we should search for the visibility of 'Self' in all these thoughts.

Brahman—the *Tattva*. In the point of view of the *Kaal* (the time), there is no beginning of the Soul and no end. In fact the Soul is beyond the motion or speed of the *Kaal* (time). The motion of the time is generated by the thought. Thought is the product of intellect. The Soul is beyond the intellect. Therefore, the Soul is beyond the boundary of *Kaal* (the time). The Soul being beyond the *Kaal* is indivisible; and the division of the pure Soul (awareness) is not possible. The awareness of the Soul is perceptible, knowable and incontrovertible. It illuminates all the three states of Jeeva; the waking state, the dreaming state and the sleeping state. The Soul knows the diversity of all the things including mind's awareness; it is infinite and one and only one—all pervading. If it is not one and imprudent, we have to consider the presence of yet another power and then both will have their limits and boundaries. Therefore all should be considered all pervading eternal entity, the Soul. The one which is omnipresent must be formless and all powerful (omnipotent) to be able to take any form. Form and name are the characteristics of the world and therefore the world is limited, exhibits changeability, destructibility and the cause of sorrow. The Soul—the Truth is formless. A formless thing has no limitations and restrictions. We cannot frame a mental picture of the Soul. Such a strange *Tattva* can be called unparalleled and consistent. This *Tattva* has two more characteristics: *Chitta* and *Anand* (bliss), meaning thereby that the Soul is unlimited wisdom and unlimited bliss. The Soul is one (singular) and unparalleled—there is no other *Tattva*. It can only be known by knowing its characteristics: (i) appearance of form and (ii) neutrality. The characteristics of appearance of form tell about the parts of object. They especially point towards particular place or action. These characteristics are impermanent. The Soul (*Tattva*) is matchless and peerless. It is identified on the basis of innate form and neutrality. *Satchittanand* (Existence-Knowledge-Bliss) is the witness of the same limitless innate form of the Soul.

'*Brahmananh yonitvat yato ba imani bhutani jayante, yen jatani jeevanti, yatra pratyavayanti*' are neutral characteristics of the Soul. These characteristics get dissolved simultaneously with the end of the era of creation and *Kaal* (time). The indistinct, inarticulate, strange growth, and development etc., are the characteristics relative to the world. Therefore the *Sadhak*, in the search of the 'Self'; (*Tattva*), should overstep the things which are not spiritual, with the help of neutral characteristics of the Soul. As he comes closer to his natural 'Self' (the Truth), he should search for the characteristics of innate form of the Soul. First, experience the power of the 'Self, thereafter divert attention towards the awareness (*Chetna*), that is, active in the power of 'Self' and then understand the bliss in awareness; experience and enjoy it. It would be a feeling of experiencing that it is the 'Self', it is the power of the 'Self', the 'Self' is like awareness. There is no difference between awareness and bliss. They are synonymous to each other. Now a search of the limits of this awareness will reveal that it is boundless, infinite, limitless. We will have the experience of the entire world and universe within ourselves. Nothing other than 'Self' will be visible. That Soul is Brahman, Shiv, *Indra* and immortal. It is self-illuminating — it is Vishnu, it is life, it is time (*Kaal*), it is fire, it is moon, it is sun. The Soul is Brahman, Ayamatma is Brahman. It is the word of *Shruti*. To be recognized in oneself, it is called *Atma* (Soul) and its all pervading expansiveness, is called Brahman. '*Servam Khalvind Brahman*' According to what is written in *Shruti*, the entire world is Brahman. One who has experienced the Soul — he witnesses everything in himself. Self knowledge leads to an understanding that I am Brahman and I am *Chetna*, which is all pervading. *Upanishads* say — *Ahm Brahmasmi*.

One who has realized Brahman, became Brahman. Awareness of The Soul and the 'Self' is immortal. Any other awareness is perishable. One which is the witness of the vision in *Upanishads*, listener of *Shruti*, knower of the knowledge, communicator of communication, the same Soul is immortal. The witness of the vision is not like a vessel. The witness and the vision are clearly different. If the witness of the vision is the vision, it must be seen all the time. It never happens that witness is not seeing the vision. Contrary to this the one who sees the vessel cannot see the vessel on becoming blind, because he is perishable. Had the vision been immortal then everyone would have had the external eye to see; but the witness of the vision being immortal, even the blind person can see the vessel in the dream. The self illuminating Existence (Being), never extinguishing Soul, is the witness of the vision. It is therefore, crystal clear that the Soul is self-illuminating and immortal. Whatever has already happened, whatever will happen in future is nothing but *Sanatan Brahman*. Only one who knows this can overstep the death. Thus, infact there is no other way to attain enlightenment. Therefore the human beings have to know the 'Self'. To be born as a human being is gift of God. It is meaningful only when he comes to know that he is the Soul and not the body. Body perishes, whereas the Soul is immortal. One gets knowledge of the 'Self' by the kindness and matchless compassion of *Sadguru* (the spiritual master). One comes to know the 'Self' through kindness of *Sadguru*. Vedanta and other scriptures have defined the Soul as inconceivable, incomprehensible. They provide teachings to think on pure Soul. It implies that thinking about the pure Soul is not at all similar to thinking about worldly objects or events or situations. In thinking about the pure Soul the meditator, the meditation and the objecting can never get satisfied. That is why the Soul is inconceivable, incomprehensible. The inconceivable does not mean that it is not knowable or its knowledge is impossible or one should not be hopeful. The Soul means that we are the 'Self' (the Soul) and the 'Self' is itself the evidence and proof. How valid and solid this proof is that the outsets are the 'witness' of our existence. What is the necessity for any proof of the 'Self' that is the Soul. The Soul is our being and we are the Soul. To think about the Soul means to think about our — 'Self'. While meditating upon the Soul we should know about existence that is 'I am the Truth', I am awareness, 'I am the bliss (*Anand*)'. We should feel our existence, awareness and bliss. Only then we can meditate upon the Soul, otherwise not. If we meditate and could not feel about our existence, our awareness and bliss; such meditation is defective and incompetent. That is not the meditation about the 'Self' that is meditating upon some state of mind. For meditation on an object, on should have a different object before himself. The object of the organs of sense can only be a thing that is visible with naked eyes. An invisible thing cannot be known by organs of sense. We ourselves are the Soul. The Soul is self illuminating; and knower and illuminator of the mind, the intellect, organs of sense and external worldly objects. For the Soul every object is visible, but the Soul is not visible to organs of sense; because both are different. The Soul is self illuminating knower and the illuminator; whereas the organs of sense are dependent on the Soul for their actions. To try to know the Soul like any visible object or even imagine the form of the Soul like any object is absolutely deceptive. It is clear that the Soul cannot be objectified. The world is like and Infinite Ocean. We see waves, bubbles, whirlpools. They originate from the water of the ocean. They all are water only. The ocean has its self existence. It is present as self in various forms. Similarly the Soul is all pervading awareness *Tattva*. It is ever existent, infinite and immortal. There is no possibility of any increment or retardation in the Soul. It is unchangeable. But it is illuminating in every object and all looks. Various names and forms in the world appear to be the parts of the same Soul. They only appear to be like delusion, imaginary but no division is possible in them with respect to the Soul. The Soul in every nook and cranny is the same. Therefore the Soul is 'Self' (*Tattva*) and the same Soul, same 'Self' and the same *Tattva* is present in different forms and names in the outer visible world. It is called different forms of the same thing. This diversity is an act of falsely or erroneously attributing the properties of one thing to another. The world is its modification alteration, changed form, alerted condition or state; and not the result or consequence or effect. Every philosopher is of the opinion that the misery or sorrow cannot be overcome if we remain in that state. The fire is the fire, how can it be cold? If we desire we cannot escape from the heat of the fire, but it is possible to change the nature of the fire. To overcome the sorrow we have invented new scientific methods but those methods have increased the terror of death and destruction. We may dream of *Satyug* — every thing in this world be good and good; but looking at the reality of the present world, it appears that it will not yield successful results. Even if we get some success, it doesn't look like we will sustain the same. In the past Ram Rajya was there and it ended. Therefore when there is sorrow and misery in all parts of the world, there could only be one solution, that is to conquer, alleviate and calm down. To live in the world without being affected by the miseries and sorrow, stay in Brahman — the creator of the world. Once we get the knowledge of Brahman, we can achieve enlightenment, otherwise not. Brahman is auspicious, Brahman is Shiv, Brahman is bliss (*Anand*). To attain knowledge of the 'Self' is the highest aim of human being. He is the enlightenment, He is the Paramanand, everlasting peace and immortal *Tattva*. Only in Him the wholeness is. He is beyond all defects and distortions. The knowledge of the 'Self' is highest knowledge and is the highest success. That state is the state of permanence tranquility and blissfulness. In this world we sometimes feel joy and happiness and we all know that how temporary it is. To attain everlasting happiness we have to achieve the knowledge of 'Self'. The Soul is immortal *Tattva*. Everyone has a desire to escape from death. Just as we all want everlasting happiness, we also want immortality of the body. But just as the desire of getting happiness is temporary, the desire of immortality of the body is temporarily wicked desire — it is the creation of ignorance. It is never possible. It is not desirable to wish for immortality of the body. It is a day dream. In fact only everlasting *Tattva* can be immortal, only the immortality of the Soul is worth meditating upon. The Soul, *Tattva* is the root of creation of the world. Brahman is the creation of the Soul *Tattva* and Brahman is the creator of the world. Thus Brahman is both the cause and instrument of the creator of the world. Some intellectuals consider the world as the creation of God. In their philosophy the Nature and the atom are the cause of creation. While considering this view, it will be seen that God becomes limited and incomplete. Therefore Brahman is both-the cause and instrument of creation. This is the principle well accepted by all scriptures. The world is the modification of Brahman. Just as a snake looks like a rope, similarly the world is visible in Brahman. The name and form of the world are unreal. The world is not the result of Brahman. The real, unique without a second, undivided, identical, same, the state of Being real, is known as the Ultimate Reality.

UNDERSTANDING OWN-SELF

Sadhana is a spiritual word. By doing *Sadhana* the *Sadhak* hopes for happiness and bliss. How to achieve happiness and bliss? In this regard spirituality and materialism have exceedingly different interpretation.

Everybody in this world is found doing many efforts to research on the desire of happiness and bliss but none could achieve permanent happiness, it disappears due to lack of satisfaction and increasing desires and wants. It is just like breaking of water bubble with the impact of the drop of water on it. When we get the desired material we feel happy. As soon as it slips away from our hands we feel distressed. Further, when we get the desired thing, the state of bliss comes in our mind for very short duration. Thereafter, a kind of agitation and distraction comes up. *'Shapen has described this situation in his words as :*

that the mind of a person wanders here and there in a state of happiness sorrow and agitation'. To remove this agitative state of mind the materialistic thinkers have expressed that we should keep on accumulating the things that provide joy and pleasure. We should remain engaged in worldly affairs and works, so that we do not get time to think about joy-sorrow. Many intellectuals on the basis of several opinions, keep the things of joy and pleasure forever.

In case of materialism, some western intellectuals have said, that such a science is the science to distract the mind. Therefore, we have to look at this world with such a psychological view point, as to whether one can search permanent happiness and bliss through *Sadhana* or by physical and material things. One who adopts *Sadhana* as a tool, is seen as mediocre by worldly people. We have seen that the *Sadhak*s unnecessarily torture their bodies to keep themselves away from worldly pleasures. Is it our folly to do like this ? What do the psychologists say in this regard ? Psychology is a science, similar to physical science. A few psychologists have original views on search of happiness. The psychologist William James has propounded the principle of *'Anand'* (bliss). He said that one can achieve *'Anand'* by thinking repeatedly on profit and desire. If one gets profits beyond his expectation, he gets more *'Anand'*. On the other hand, if the expectation and desire are high and the profits are less then the degree of *'Anand'* will also be of a lesser order. The degree of *'Anand'*can be increased by internally reducing the expectations and desires. If the profits are exceedingly high the '*Anand*' be of much greater heights; that could be termed as '*Brahmanand*'. This is clearly proved by simple mathematics of desire and expectations. It is a psychological equation mathematically found to hold good.

One who possesses right, proper, good, auspicious, skillful, proficient, well-versed intellect, will have the clear vision of this truth. Now the question is, how to achieve the zeroing of expectations? It is not easily achievable. Everyone in the world has told about the fact that in absence of desires and expectations '*Anand*' is achievable. *Sadhana* is essential to achieve void in regard to desires and expectations. Desires and expectations are the waves of the mind. The mind is disturbed by desires and expectations. The peaceful mind is devoid of desires and expectations. To attain peaceful state of mind, it is essential to practice *Sadhana* continuously. The mind moves very fast like wind, but by practice and renunciation it can be brought under control. In '*Yogadarshan*' Maharishi Patanjali has said : '*Abhyas vairagyabhayam tannirodhah*' meaning thereby practice takes a man towards perfection. The lion that is caged for several years does not run away, even when the cage is opened. The prisoners who spend a major portion of their life in the prison, when released, again wish to go to the prison. Those who consistently and continuously work in dark mines, pass their lives happily and it is only due to practice that those who live on volcanic hills pass their life without fear. Similarly aeroplane pilots take the flight without fear. Such persons can lose their lives any moment, but they do not worry about it. It is due to practice that mathematicians achieve such a concentration that they forget about the activities of their body. The mind can be controlled by practice in such a way that it becomes friendly and agreeable. It could start living in the situations one wants. Repeatedly continuous practice brings concentration in mind and in the concentration one starts experiencing '*Anand*'. Therefore to make any situation good depends upon practice (*Sadhana*). If our mind is in our control, we can enjoy every situation with happiness. The mind undoubtedly can be kept under control by practice. There are different types of practice to achieve control over mind. These practices are termed as *Sadhana*. The man who has unsmeared himself from happiness-unhappiness, honor-dishonor, peace-perplexed, can always remain stablizied in peaceful state. The person who can tolerate and withstand the impulse and force of desire and anger, is the deserving candidate for real bliss.

When we prepare our mind in advance to tolerate the sorrows and miseries, we do not waiver, fickle, deviate and get perturbed. In this world no situation always remains the same. The situations are always changing. Only the *Sadhak*s who remain fearless in these changes and unfavourable conditions do not waiver and tremble under them, can enjoy oneness and happiness. Only such a *Sadhak* can meditate upon

71

spiritual *Tattva* (the Truth). To know the truth, it is not possible to meditate upon mind. Therefore, the practice to have control over the mind, is the only way to know the Truth. So many *Yati*, *Sanyasi* (One who has completely renunciated the world and its possessions and attachments) and the *Sadhak*s (the seekers of the Truth) practice *Hath Yoga* (abstract meditation, the science of forced meditation) to achieve control over the mind. The people of modern civilization laugh at such *Sadhak*s. Such efforts, they consider, as the indicator of poor intellect. However, if we go through the life sketch of the seekers of the Truth and look into their inner life, we will find that in view of psychological analysis, *Hath Yoga* is also a right path. One great saint, a *Tattva Vetta*, 'Dayojneej (who was the disciple of Sukrat) could keep himself away from his fame, due to his practice of *Hath Yoga*. Once, a young person saw him begging from a stone idol. He enquired from him, 'Hey Gentleman, knowing fully well that what can a stone idol give as Alm, you are begging form a stone idol'. Dayojneej replied. 'I am begging from a stone idol to practice to keep myself in a state of peace, in the event of begging from a person if I do not get the Alm.' In fact begging is a tool of Yogis for renunciation. There are many things by which hunger can be met with, but begging attitude is one of the strong and powerful part of *Sadhana*, when one gets the opportunity to read fame-insult, honor dishonor and inner duality. The Yogi whose *Chitta* wavers, fickles and becomes unsteady under these conditions often go down. Ramakrishna Paramhans used to practice Takka-Maati (money-soil). In one hand he used to keep coin money and in the other the soil, and go on repeating Takka-Maati, Takka-Maati and then threw both in the river Ganga. This type of practice saves a person from the greed of money. Many saints have practiced to remain uninfluenced by the world in many ways. Swami Ramteerth had a special liking for a few fruits. Those fruits used to drag his mind in that direction. Even in his deep meditative state his mind used to travel in that direction. One day he brought those fruits and kept them in front of himself, so he may see them all the time. What happened, you know. The mind travelled repeatedly towards those fruits and Swami Ramteerth dragged it back to himself every time. This inner conflict continued for some days. The fruits rotted and tasted bad. Swami ji, threw those fruits in Ganga river. Swami ji told that the result of this practice was that his desire for those fruits vanished for ever. So, there are many types of practices to have control over the mind. *Hath Yoga* is therefore an effective tool to obtain control over the mind. But one must remember that in *Hath Yoga*, thought process, discriminative power, knowledge about the impermanence non-reality of things are important aspects, otherwise the *Hath Yoga* will become unfruitful. There will be no feeling of any advancement in *Sadhana*. Besides *Hath Yoga* there are other methods of controlling the mind. Modern analysts of *Chitta* have scientifically discovered some valuable information that show that *Hath Yoga* is not good for mental health. There is a possibility that those who practice *Hath Yoga* can become victim of mental and physical illness. Therefore, some of the pschycologists say that the resistance to our behavior is harmful; but it is their great misconception and mistake to formulate the things in this manner. The knot, distortion, falsehood, or perversion of the Truth are generated by resisting those desires and feelings that are supressed by thoughtlessness. Without understanding, where there is a thoughtful effort to control the desire, there is no possibility of creation of any knot or perversion in the mind. The desires that are not fulfilled due to unfavorable conditions and environment, appear as dream and intense passion or insanity. A willing self-control is not at all a destructive element. Some intellectuals say that an analysis of *Chitta* and the discoveries of science can reveal that one who disobeys the order of the moral intellect may suffer from mental and physical diseases. If any kind of transgression is against our moral intellect, though satisfying our animal instinct, it, is bound to bring turbulence and agitation in the mind. Our moral intellect will always be telling us about transgression and we cannot stay at peace. The sin is troublesome and the righteousness is pleasant. This statement contains psychological truth. The mind can be controlled in many ways; some of them are : (I) to change the direction of its movement and (ii) to make it motionless. In *Yoga Darshan*, it is written that the motionless state of mind is the aim of practicing *Yoga*.

> *'Yogaschittavratti nirrodhah tadraa*
> *drashtuh swaroope avasthanam'*

As soon as *Chitta-Vratti* gets negated and becomes motionless, the 'Self' gets revealed. *Sadhana* of *Ashtang Yoga* takes one to profound meditative state, *Savikalp Samadhi*, where he can recognize the distinction between the subject and the object, the knower and the known. The meditative state where the distinction between the knower and known disappears (*Nirvikalp Samadhi*) is beyond the former state (*Savikalpa Samadhi*). According to psychological science, it is not possible to bring the mind to a motionless state. Just as a moving vehicle needs to be stopped slowly, similarly the mind is to be made motionless slowly and slowly. If the moving vehicle is stopped suddenly, it wavers and loses balance. So is the case with the mind. This truth is well understood by musicians. In *Gita*, *Bhakti Yoga* and *Karma Yoga* have been told as the best approach to control the mind. Both the traditions of worship, God with attributes and God without attributes are praise-worthy. However, God has told that it is easier to control the mind through worshiping him as Brahman with attributes. When only one and the same *Tattva* is pervading in the entire world and universe, offering services to Him is to attain Brahman. If we are atheist, it is useless to bring any other feeling in the mind. We should use our

75

mind in worthy tasks. All actions are the actions of the same *Tattva* that is omnipresent, omnipotent and omniscient. Having come to know this truth, whatever we do is to serve Him. (God)

knowledge he has gained. Maharashi Vashishta has considered action and knowledge as two wings of a bird (Yoga Vashishta). The man cannot progress and succeed only by *Karma* (action) or by knowledge alone. A good knowledge truly provides the right direction for *Karma* (action) and enhances the pure potential for doing work. Any good work provides incremental effect in obtaining new knowledge. Every good work is responsible for enhancement of Spiritual knowledge. Whenever there is loss of balance between action and knowledge, that is whenever there is dominance of either of these two, an uneven mental state is created. This is the state of mental sickness. The men who remain busy in worldly *Karma* (action), they lose their potential strength for Spiritual thinking. Such people start measuring their success on the basis of external results. As they achieve success in the world out there, they go further forward. Considering the success in outside world as a measure of advancement in life, increases the ego. The man, then forgets the spiritual aspects of his success. Under such a situation, there is retardation in subtle vision and the man becomes liable to commit various kinds of mistakes. Due to various mistakes committed, man continues his outward journey and does not make any attempt to go within. He starts blaming others for his failures. When the man looks at the faults of others, his friend circle gets affected and he creates more enemies, instead of friends. In case of prevalence of worldly vision, while doing any work many kind of doubts come into the mind. Due to the doubts, man is not able to do any work with full attention and expriences dejection, hopelessness all around. Such a person lacks enthusiasm and becomes passive towards activities. If the man is aware of the past experience of his activities, he starts finding reasons for his failure. Renunciating his ego, he surrenders himself to any of greatest truth and gets a new enthusiasm. If one's past experience is contrary to the spirituality, he calls for death in the event of his failure in worldly affairs. As a result, whatever one thinks within gets manifested outside, meaning thereby that he becomes destructive for himself. Just as action alone is not competent enough for progressive succession of life, similarly without action knowledge is devoid of experience. Knowledge devoid of practical experience is bookish knowledge. Actions purify mental feelings. In absence of this balance, the thought process gets filled with hopelessness, negativity and darkness. One is not able to concentrate on any single issue and he sees all the visible points full of faults. He starts feeling deception and illusion in every thing. He is not satisfied with any principle of life. Under such conditions he feels compelled to be passive towards spiritual thinking. Just as in lack of spiritual thinking one loses his self-confidence, similarly, in absence of actions, one who is always engaged in spiritual thinking does not get potential advantage of knowledge. The higher knowledge is that knowledge which stands on the ground of experience. This experience comes through various circumstances, contacts with people and behavioral practice. The man who deliberately does not do any work, ultimately is compelled to do some work by himself. The worldly people have attachment for eating, drinking merry-making and acting. Only a few have inclination towards spirituality. Action-attached people are to be told about the essentiality of work. More than that they are to be told about keeping affection and love for knowledge.

By spiritual thinking man achieves the knowledge of original strength and power lying within. Success in action and work comes when man gets full knowledge of 'Self' i.e. mental powers and strength. The more one thinks and meditates on his mental powers, the more he gets the knowledge of the strength of those mental powers.

How strong is the power of thought process? It is difficult to reckon when man measures the power of his thought process on the basis of outer success; he commits a big mistake.

The work that we can do in outer world, accounts for a very small part of our ability to do real work. How much energy, strength and power does a man possess? He himself is unaware of the same. He considers his small success as a big success and ultimately he loses that too. A man's power to do work depends on his self-confidence and the self-confidence is a result of spiritual thought process. The man who concentrates his mind on the duty in the present and uses the remainder strength on spiritual thinking, never loses his self-confidence. The man who thinks too much about pros and cons of every work, going into past and future, wastes a lot of energy working uselessly, such a person loses his self-confidence and consequently his capacity to work reduces. He starts committing mistakes quite often. This represents a disbalanced mind, and indicates the necessity of spiritual thinking. When the man gets inflated on his achievements and starts planning for very big projects, he loses his balance of mind. The plans create various types of worries and doubts. In this manner his thinking of pros and cons consumes his mental energy in useless aspects. Success becomes the cause of failure. Spiritual thinking is the best way to combat worries. When the man starts making whole hearted efforts to know the unchanging *Tattva* (the Truth, EEE), he does not give much importance to the future. Spiritual thinking becomes his priority. In this way, the above mentioned events do not agitate and disturb the man. When the man is at peace, he can do much more work in comparison to his unpeaceful state of mind. The man spends his energy unnecessarily in worrying about unfavorable future events. The man destroys his mental energy to a great extent in emotional modifications and contemplation of fear, doubt and unwillingness. Due to fear of the future, the man discards his duties of the present and excessively worries about his future. The spiritual thinking teaches the man to live in the present and to get rid of fear. The spiritual thinking directs the man towards the Truth, the Everlasting Eternal Existence, the *Tattva*, (Brahman) the Ultimate Reality, the Absolute. The reason for retardation of the energy in the man is his personal worries. When the aim of the activities undertaken by the man is for a great cause, without any ulterior motive of his own, his mind does not waiver. Neither he gets excited nor agitated by temporary success or failure, respectively. The man who aims to work for the welfare of all has enormous capacity, ability, skill and power to work. The man is not able to focus on his work that would result in the welfare of all others, until and unless, he creates oneness with his inner-self and all pervading *Tattva*, that is, Brahman (EEE). When one starts feeling that his own welfare is included in the welfare of all others and thinks that only such a feeling and action can give him real peace, then and only then, discarding his own selfishness, applies his mind for the work that are beneficial to all others. He undertakes great jobs with full determination and planning. To do so, it is essential to perform spiritual practices continuously. Until and unless the man understands that by helping others, he not only gets worldly benefits but also attains internal wholeness, it is not possible for him to take up the projects for the welfare of others. Those who get away from spiritual thinking and remain busy in worldly affairs, get easily delighted on their success. They start looking at themselves as philanthropist. In such a situation, they expect praise from others and want people to follow them. Such persons think themselves elite and try to convince others that they are great. This egoistic nature create several enemies for them. They lose their credibility as social worker. They mutilate any opposition to what they think as correct and good. Their obstinacy and stubbornness takes them towards destruction. Without spiritual thinking, the man cannot have the feeling of discipline and modesty. The capability for self-improvement is greatly reduced. He becomes vulnerable and often commits mistakes. In this way he makes his life a failure. Spiritual thinking is therefore a must. Spiritual thinking means to discover the Truth, that is the never changing *Tattva* (EEE).

EGOTISM

Human life is streaming forth by an unique orderly arrangement. The arrangements do exist in the outer world, but if we look deeply it will be seen that the mental activities of human being also flow in a cyclic arrangement. Man is bound with an arrangement. Bound with a particular arrangement system. The life of human being has become like a mechanical investment. Human and super human activities and internal reactions are seen like a stable and balanced arrangement. Why and due to what it is happening? The human being is ignorant about it. This ignorance is because of lack of awareness. In lack of awareness, he is deprived of success despite concerted efforts.

Why we cannot be cautious about such type of inner reactions ? The moment we begin our inner journey, every corner of our body will attain pace to attack, surpass and overcome the mechanical way of living. Our existence will be keen, to unfold the 'Self'. We should therefore be consciously aware of our every action.

Our thought process, over imitating actions and our many types of reactions leave their impression on our mind. The person gets fascinated by his own nature. He gets caged into self-made prison and is bounded by the convictions arrived at self-created reactions. All this, is happening slowly and slowly, unknowingly the person gets used to a set kind of activity and arrangement and it is nothing but a type of dense unconsciousness.

Accidently without any effort, when this kind of fascination breaks and adequate awareness wakes up, the man feels that there is some bondage. If there is some bondage, it must be opened. How these bondages have entered into the mind ? Why we accepted them ? When they could find their opportunity to enter into ? When any of these questions ask for the clearing of the doubt, then our entire flow of life will look for purification. We must also know that; what we do not cherish, why it is coming back ? Try to understand, who is the thinker ? You will come to know that you are not the thinker. You are the witness of the thought. This perfection will come all of a sudden in a flash of moment, and this perception proves that whatever is happening is not likeable. When we, as a witness of thought, find that we are agitated, excited and are the witness of the same; it will ascertain that whatever we have seen, heard and experienced is the casting and hushing of external things and matter. These castings are continuously becoming

Samskara (impressions) and due to which the thought is getting influenced.

Thought process, the touch and contact of inner and outer impressions give rise to a balanced vision. Our intent or vision towards worldly things and objects is the same as already existing in the impressions. In the inner turmoil and in the middle of chaos and crowd of thought and determination, what is happening in me ? We must see courageously.

Awareness is the most important achievement of a *Sadhak* (spiritual seeker). The awareness helps in ignoring the thought. Going deep into the origin of the activity of thought and touching the strength and power of the thought, the inner chaos calms down and unwanted things are broken and destroyed with the awakening of the 'Self', meaning thereby that on becoming the witness of the inner-self, everything vanishes, thoughts get submerged, the activities disappear and reactions, as if, have gone to sleep. Then what remains, the whole, the entire, the complete, the perfect. In this state of wholeness or the entirety, the remainder is the 'Self' (the Soul); it is not the impression, not the casting.

To be a witness is to know, who am I ? What is happening in me ? By keeping a balanced state in continuous attack and impact of thought process and activity, it can be understood that the thought process is the activity that does not allow us to remain in a balanced state. If we can effectively and cautiously see into the middle of thought disappearance and appearance, it will be possible to stay calm during the period that generates anxiety, uneasiness and agitation. Inner conflicts can also be subsided.

Be alert, be cautious! You will not do anything, you will only be a witness to all this and with total awareness, will try to see all this as witness of the 'Self' in presence of 'Self'. Only in this way we can see the disappearance of the impressions. Otherwise our impressions can take any form of ego. The egotism crushes all our possibilities. The flowers that bloom in a state of being witness get dried up, when we think that we are the doer. We are not the doer. Whenever we call us as doer, we are giving the opportunity to our ego to destroy our state of being witness. There are many entry points of ego. Many times it enters wearing beautifully dressed politeness and many times it does unpious acting of the purity of forgiveness. We should always try to recognize the bare habits of our egotism. If we can do this honestly, the deep feeling of being a witness will certainly build-up. An innocent and pure state will appear, like a shrine. It may be difficult but not impossible. We must break self-fascination. On breaking down self-fascination, one will achieve a state like that of a shrine. A temple-like environment is created, where worship and *Sadhana* and all become meaningful and significant. It is therefore essential to be adequately aware and wakeful.

UNDERSTANDING EXPERIENCING THE TRUTH

The Truth by itself is our Nature. The Truth manifests in the mind which is void of knowledge/wisdom. The Truth is revealed in the absence of our knowledge, i.e. when our knowledge is not involved in any action. Mind is a house of knowledge. Truth is the remainder of knowledge. When this house of knowledge becomes void and whatever is seen and heard is left out, then the manifestation that takes place has the ability and capability to reveal the Truth. It is essential that we for our mind, for the conscious and unconscious experiences of the past, and for our activities and reactions must always remain conscious. We cannot achieve the Truth through any one else. How can it be? The truth is neither a gross thing nor object, place or reaction, nor distantly available anxiety. The Truth is live, dynamic, awareness, inspiration, the Supreme Spirit, essence of all being, source of all sensation.

He is not even the *Sadhak*. Had the Truth been fixed place point, it would not have existed as the Truth; it would have become merely a material property. When the mind research for finding the Truth, projects itself to look it in outer world, adopting traditional techniques, symbolic activities and pre-conceived notions. While finding the Truth the mind thus starts searching self-impressions. Ultimately, due to idealistic self-impressions, the mind accepts the unreal. This process of research does not lead to realization of the Real. The Real is what really exists permanently. There is nothing against the permanent Ultimate Reality. When the entire knowledge disappears, the sweet experience of EEE is nothing but the Truth. We can only think about knowledge and run for the knowledge. When the mind is not knowledge, results of knowledge and activities and reactivities based on knowledge, the Truth reveals itself like a Real and permanent entity.

The problem is to know what is Real in us? In the midst of various experiences, deciding our aim, our own thoughts impressions are projected, casted and thrown forward. After all what is that, we are searching for? What is that, which every one wants? Especially in this unpeaceful world, where everyone is making efforts for comfort and shelter to get happiness. It is essential to know about the same. In the absence of the Truth, it may prove to be deceptive like a mirage. Can we come across the Truth instantly without making any preparation? Yes, by becoming aware of our own immitative activities, our own motives and our own creations, if we care for them, we can understand our role. We must not fear our problems. A proper looking over the problems will definitely provide the solution. Every problem contains the solution in itself. There is no such quiz which does not have the solution. Every question has its hidden answer in itself. What am I ? Who am I ? does not need any proof from anyone else. For the proof for the 'Self', any other proof is meaningless. The 'Self' is the proof for the 'Self'. The help to the search for the proof of the 'Self' will prove to be proofless in itself.

The existence of ourselves, that we know, is casted in many ways. We want to know the 'Self' in conjunction with our past deeds, traditional bondages and many other pre-conceived ideas and convictions, but this proves to be an incomplete knowledge. When our knowledge gets dissolved in silence, the vision of the Truth will enlighten us with its sharp rays. Just as in the absence of light nothing is visible; similarly in the absence of the knowledge about the Truth the meaning of life becomes dull and hazy. But as the Sun-like Truth is revealed, the life becomes new and purposeful and it becomes pure like a temple. The Truth is simple and blissful in itself. When we discard the Truth and put on other masks, we are found running away from the Truth. Our difficulty is that without knowing that why we do present unreal, yet we present unreal. It is our helplessness (having lost control over oneself); and simply we destroy our pure natural state. We have to save ourselves from such a dual life. Many streams of thought, thinking and nature keep us busy in making our outer world glamorous and beautiful and continuously inspire us to remain entangled in it, whereas actually we want something else. We should go deep to recognize our inner-personality, which is hidden behind the mask worn by us and look at its bare nature.

In this process when concentration on the inner-resolution and dissolution of mind make inner-self bare, obstructions will get broken and one can come to his inner-self.

In the inner-self a stream of casted thought process, activities and reactivities are flowing. It is self deception. Should not we be alert towards ourselves? How will you know? First you should get rid of all those elements which are obstructive; meaning thereby, every expectation, every desire of permanence, the inquisitiveness of what is elsewhere — because the mind in the wish of continuous security wants security for its existence. The security is nothing but self-control. The existence of the 'Self' fills us with the own 'Self'.

ATTENTIVENESS TO BE VIGILANT

The *Sadhak* attains a state to experience the 'Self, provided he is attentive, vigilant and aware throughout. Even if the *Sadhak* cannot remain attentive for a long time, he should not leave his *Sadhana*. Try only to observe, and how we become insensible at every step should catch our attention towards this senselessness. The *Sadhak*'s attentiveness towards failures can make him vigilant. It is not that the *Sadhak* does not possess the ability to become what he wants to become, but the main obstacle is his inattentiveness. When the *Sadhak* with a tranquil mind is proficient and wise in his behavior, he gradually attains the state, which he could not attain in early stages. Deep attentiveness, nice expected behavior, well proven thought about the Truth and by right understanding, the *Sadhak* comes to know everything that he wants to know.

What the *Sadhak* is in the present, is the same as he wanted to be. In this Truth, the greater the fixity, firmness and steadiness, the greater will be the equanimity, balance, sharpness, intellect and increment in the working skill. The *Sadhak*'s state of stillness of the mind for long period in such a natural state is going to make him free from pleasure of senses. The result of action will then easily be acceptable to the everlasting eternal existence (EEE), the 'Self'. Divine attributes like enviouslessness, agelessness, desirelessness and simplicity, etc. will begin to develop in the *Sadhak* and he will get filled with the presence of unutterable godly bliss (*Anand*). In the absence of desire, worry etc., all the efforts of the *Sadhak* will get diverted towards God. The experience of this eternal law will be easily understandable, just like the knowledge that if we drop any thing from the roof it will fall down. We know this very well. Therefore we do not worry and wait and desire anything.

When the behavior of the *Sadhak* is full of worship and adoration, all his efforts and action get arranged and concerted to recognize the Truth, an explosion takes place for which the *Sadhak* was waiting since long. This explosion is absolutely peaceful. The *Sadhak* has the only right that he must identify the reality in every condition. With this simple practice (*Sadhana*), he will get God's blessings and power to destroy his ego. He will also come to know that he has to do nothing but to live purity, as a witness and thinking the 'Self' as Supreme Spirit. Politely addressing, spirituality is not labour oriented. It is also not a complicated, complex, difficult and troublesome path. It is such a path where you accept yourself as you are (under any circumstances) without depriving the Truth. Now there is a question. Are all other things useless? No; but they are not as true as the Eternal Truth is. In front of the experience of the *Sanatan* law of action-cause, all our victories and attributes and astonishing achievements are mean. For the persons who have come to know the experiences of this eternal law and all mysteries about it, the materialistic slogans and their achievements are nothing but bare.

In the advancement or downfall of man, the basic foundation is his thought process and its successful actions, imitations, reactions. Expectations of victory, prosperity, plenty and achievements are a part of the nature of man and due to this nature, the major portion goes in being extravagant in meaningless efforts. There could be no avoidance towards rise, success, prosperity, elevation, success; but passivity towards righteousness makes us aimless. Useless thinking and meaningless actions will definitely yield obstacles and inauspicious and unfavorable results. It becomes a dense hinderence for future efforts. In order to touch the highest peak of greatness, the *Sadhak* in conjunction with healthy thinking must lift up and uprise his convictions.

Being always conscious about the aim, pure thinking process filled with perception as witness in selecting purified surroundings, we can permanently get into an auspicious and blessed state. When will it be accomplished?, the *Sadhak* should not worry.

Experiencing spiritual accomplishments is a certainty and the *Sadhak* gets encouragement and enthusiasm. These experiences generate a feeling of love in the *Sadhak* and create a fertile ground for truthful devotional commitment. The *Sadhak* should keep all his experiences secret and continue treading the spiritual path enthusiastically.

The more you delay, the more harmful it will be. One should spend patiently the time required for spiritual quest. The *Sadhak* really does not know, the damage that useless thinking, useless efforts and crying do. One should not again and again change the resources used for concentration (*Mantra*, objects, etc.) The orderly practice performed seriously takes to the center of our source. When we practice with pure heart and keen desire to achieve the aim, all the cosmic forces come to help. What we have to do, is to concentrate patiently with godly feeling in our *Sadhana* (spiritual practice).

INNATE NATURE

To be expansive and whole, the *Sadhak* must give up his mean narrowness. Only by discarding his meanness, he can go forward towards the Supreme to attain wholeness. The *Sadhak* is naturally required to practice in the direction to seeking wholeness in onself rather than waiting to see wholeness in others. It will be the first step towards wholeness.

This type of transformation is the base of real progress and original advancement. The *Sadhak* for his own development must not wait for others development. This type of expectation or hope will prove to be very dear to him. During his inner journey the *Sadhak* comes to know, that he is not as great as others consider. Generally we look at the faults of others and ignore or avoid their entire greatness. Therefore a traveler who cares for others, should avoid finding faults in others and carry on continuous introspection. In the 'Self' one is great beyond doubt but must not show his greatness in conduct or behavior.

Man is the all powerful master of every state of his inmate nature, but he has forgotten this everlasting truth. To be all powerful is his innate natural state, but he has forgotten to be the same.

Man in his equability or sameness is Deva (god) and also whole. On being conscious about this *Sanatan* and Eternal Truth, man will find store of infinite energy and power in himself. Mahrishis, learned and enlightened persons have experienced infinite power, capacity, ability, strength and competence in man. Therefore the *Sadhak* has to make those shining eternal strengths, a live ground and base to exhibit dormant Brahman.

Introspection even once, means to have a feel of matchless-capacious power, infinite energy and eternal light. A number of powers of our inner-self are eagerly waiting for their exposition. Many virtues, good thoughts, good attitude and good mental resolve are bubbling to come out from inner-self, the moment we become conscious about the 'Self'. The seeds start germinating and then our entire mental live energy and accomplishments, filling our consciousness in the presence of the 'Self' with fragrance, prompt us for a divine, great, noble and generous course of living. To attain this state we need not leave or renounce anything, nor do we have to hate or avoid anyone, because all come from the same source, advait or oneness. We are the expansion of the same Brahman (Supreme Spirit).

The man sees division in objects and matters, but in reality there is no division. We are the waves of one and the same ocean. The water of one and the same ocean is contained in different shapes and forms of pots, objects, matters, made of different material and every shape and form has its own importance. Therefore often outside vision is like a mirage. Inhere is the same as outthere. The gross and conscious both contains the same. Therefore, by awakening pure mental resolve we should breath at all places to inhale non deceptivity, fearlessness, freedom (choicelessness), divine sweetness and beauty and encourage others to do the same. In this way the intense darkness will start disappearing by itself and everything will start illuminating in oneself.

In such a state what you experience, covering all your knowledge and wisdom, will fill you with divine compassion and love. Then you will become a resource for the auspiciousness and welfare of people. You will become absolutely pure like piousness of all pilgrimages and their worship and divine peacefulness of planets Divine purity is our innate nature.

Alert and well versed great people have made concerted efforts to see life and understand one 'Purush' (Brahman), one Soul and one personality at every stage of life. The same one 'Purush' was divided into four parts:

(i) Mind (Brahmin)
(ii) Arms (Kshatriya)
(iii) Stomach (Vaishya)
(iv) Legs (Shudra)

In this way while being one in the inborn one's originality, personal and social life was seen in four forms-Brahama has four mouths, there are four Vedas, there are four arms of Lord Vishnu. Infinite deepness is hidden in the meaning of these aspects. Like this the exposition of works of a person was divided into four castes and four '*Ashram*' (dwelling place).

The following forms four residence in the same heaven with any deity, intimate union especially into a deity, nearness or vicinity with any deity, and perfect isolation (exclusiveness) are fixed for the worship of '*Purush*'. The purpose of human life has also been divided into four: *Dharma, Artha, Kaama* and *Moksha*.

This is called oneness in manyness and the way of life after knowing the Supreme One.

The numerous manifestations having different forms and nature and following different *panthas* (religions) represent oneness and He is making it evident in every nook and cranny living or non-living. The *Sadhak* should always try to make real efforts with love to connect himself with the One (Brahman) omnipresent, omnipotent and omniscient. To reach upto Him Is Divinity.

INNATE INQUIRY
NATURALLY

To know the 'Self' means an understanding about the whole and relationship between the world and one-self. This relationship is not restricted to person alone, it should be with the nature as well and with those things that are in our rights. Individuality or singleness or distributive pervasion is dependent on the whole. The life is a subject of inter-connectedness or inter-relationship. This relationship is dynamic. To know this dynamic relationship such an innate inquiry naturally is essential. With devotionally sensitive worship it becomes purified. Thereafter discipline, actionlessness, practice and vigilance are not required. The *Sadhak* not only makes innate inquiry every moment, during wake-up state, about his thought process and sensitivities, but also does the same in the 'Self'. During this activity of innate inquiry he discards all symbolics naturally; and while going deep into the process, it is revealed that what we transform into dream, also get detached and dissolved. In this manner one opens the door to expose the unknown to become known. However to get into unknown he has to go beyond the door, because what is unknown, is the Truth. Our difficulty is that we fear to jump into unknown.

The Truth is not like an object that we can know. What can be known can never be the Truth. The mind itself is the result of known and unknown, the past that cannot be reached beyond the cognizance of senses.

It is therefore essential for the mind to understand itself and its actions, and it is possible only when the unknown gets exposed or perceived. In all these activities innate inquiry naturally is essential and in the state of innate enquiry, the experiences that the *Sadhak* will have, without accumulating them, he should remain alert every moment to make innate inquiry for their symbolic forms. In fact the *Sadhak*'s innate inquiry is tied with accumulation of the experiences and in such a state of accumulation, inspection is not possible; rather there is transformation. Where there is transformation, there is mental resolve (volition, purpose, aim, intention, determination); otherwise determination creates complexity. No doubt that we should make unconditional innate enquiry. If we are aware even for a moment, we can understand it.

Innate inquiry means that while introspecting our every thought and every activity, we do not avoid them and discard them; but along with every activity, impression and reactivity we must introspect that object of action naturally. With such a natural state, the importance of organs of senses and object will start getting revealed. It may appear to be a prohibitive state or actionlessness. But certainly it is such an activity, that naturally we come to know about the indicative form of our relationships.

How should we proceed for innate inquiry? First we become aware about our reactions on any anxiety. For example, when we look at a bunch of flowers, we get a reaction. Therefore sensitivity, touch, connection, intimacy and desire, respectively, come up. In this manner we get joy/sorrow on intimate connection and our intellect lies in recognizing the joy and avoiding the sorrow. If we have a liking for something and it provides joy an immediate response to this truth comes out in accordance to our own competence and if it provides sorrow and pain, the development of confidence to safe guard ourselves begins. To understand and know oneself does not depend on competence. It is not a technique that you learn, practice continuously, preserve and develop in your period of work. The examination of awareness to understand the 'Self' can only be done through working on inter-connectedness and mutual relationship. This can be examined by our behavior, as to how alert we are about the 'Self'. The *Sadhak* must remain alert towards his 'Self'. The *Sadhak* is required to examine himself without comparison, intimacy and avoidance or neglect. In this state, the *Sadhak* ends unconscious, relinquishing his unconcious activities. Most unconscious activities become automatically inactive. In this activity, remaining aware for all the purposes, the *Sadhak* should remain alert with full faith towards the Truth; then and only then the *Sadhak* can become Supreme.

INTERNAL OPPOSITION

Today the life has become extraordinarily complicated. Any effort made to visualize the life does not yield adequate results. The life appears to be scattered and extensively involved in a number of issues. Even efforts and activities do not help. Man finds inward obstruction (internal opposition) in his outward life. This inward obstruction is happening every moment and we are feeling lack of satisfaction and peace. This feeling is not only in one person but it is seen all over. The state of inward obstruction is the continuous state of rejection or acceptance of what we want to be or what we are. It is a clear-cut truth strife. This internal opposition is a big battle, and strife of infinite group of warriors attack us and bring us to a state of helplessness. The life is not as easy as we have considered. Life is an extraordinarily inter-twined knot, unsolved quiz and such a current in which we continuously flow, entangle ourselves and see our 'Self' away from our 'Self'. What is our internal opposition?; it is essential for the *Sadhak* to know. It is beyond doubt, the circumstrances do not remain the same all the time. All the time the ambitions and desire to become something and their exposition are generated in the mind. And when they want to come into a visible form, internal opposition comes up. This clearly indicates that one type of temporary state is being obstructed by the other temporary state. In order to prove our superiority, exhibition of our achievements and establishment of our headship lead to a kind of state of helplessness.

The cause of the birth of such a state of helplessness is internal opposition. Therefore, it is essential to watch the result of various activities with perfect equanimity. It may happen that the struggle in the state of internal opposition inspires us. In order to understand the entire purpose and importance of life, it is essential that we must understand its entire internal arrangement order and sequence. We ourselves are responsible for our own state and condition. We ourselves are creating unpleasantness and extraordinary complexity in our lives. To attain peace, it is not necessary to condemn the past. Vigilance of internal opposition and innate inquiry naturally will clear the present position. Reincarnation is only possible in the present. Reconstruction and rearrangement is possible only in the present. The formation of falsehood in ourselves can be clearly seen during innate inquiry and consequently internal opposition will become calm and quite. In this activity introspection is the first helpful element. The *Sadhak* in the state of internal opposition, in the absence of required awakening, has to free himself from the activity of self-enclosure or surrounding or circumference. Otherwise inter-connectivity will not create equanimity. To get out we should start from the nearest. Avoidance of the nearest will not let you get out. The *Sadhak* usually tries for long jump and that is not a useful jump. Although there is no difference between near and far, rather there is no distance; the beginning and the end are the same. The shape and the end are the same. The shape and the forms of the beginning, being different, yet they are the same. The end is always the same.

We should keep ourselves free from complexity. The complexity expands the ego and diminishes our spiritual grace, magnificence and splendor. The complexity disturbs our innate natural state and many strifes create new indolence or stupidity or laziness or dullness. Therefore remaining alert about the inner-reactions reduces internal opposition. Thought process is never able to conclude or terminate the thoughts. The source of thought process lies in between the 'Self' and the 'Highest'. Can we know the 'Self'? Definitely, Yes; but by its analysis. By seeing the thing or object in its original state, not as a principle, but as a practical Truth. Getting aware about it without expectation of any result and understanding its inaction we can know the 'Self' in reality; and this knowledge will finish internal opposition and give birth to never ending peace and happiness. Only in a peaceful state we can unfold the 'Self' and this is the supreme path to move towards the Supreme.

MENTAL VISION –
STATE OF MIND

Just as a pure and pious river, before dissolving and submerging its existence (entity) into expansive, deep and infinite ocean bearing many obstructions created by the company of hilly forests, many gardens and forests, many beds of rocks, demon-like large and unbreakable stone rocks, continuously pours itself courageously into ocean, similarly the *Sadhak*, in whom the worldly desires or passions are absent, continuously make efforts to connect himself with the 'Supreme' using his entire '*Sattavic Energy*', blessings of '*Sadguru*' and inspiration of God. The 'Supreme' (God) is unchangeable Everlasting Eternal Existence. We are always connected with Him but to know we have to face many obstructions, resistances and troubles. When our entire awareness and energy is placed towards the 'Supreme, hinderances in many forms come before us. The *Sadhak* with his discriminative power getting acquainted with the forms of those obstructions and hinderances enthusiastically works to make his 'Self' firmly attached to the 'Self' (Supreme)

There are four kinds of impediments: adherence, confusion, passion and joyous taste. Mental vision due to laziness, rejects, avoids and cheats the pleasure of words and worldly objects; but by not seeing the appearance of the balanced form of awareness, becomes quiet. Often appearance of such kind of state is called adherence.

The mental vision comes forward to get, achieve and accept indivisible object but is not able to absorb the same and again gets engaged with words and worldly objects as described by words. It is called confusion. The mental vision of the *Sadhak* is blocked up with polluting and corrupting blemishes of attachment. Under such a state, despite the absence of adherence and confusion, the *Sadhak*'s mental vision is unable to absorb the abstract thing. This type of impediment is called passion. God's compassion, *Sadguru*'s kindness and selfless hardwork of the *Sadhak* creates a *Chitta* devoid of all hurdles, akin to innate state where the light exists undisturbed. Only under such a state the *Sadhak* can attain an exclusive concentration upon the one entity without distinct and separate consciousness of the knower, the known and the knowing and without even self consciousness. In this condition the

Sadhak feels himself attached to the Supreme and the net work of all the alternatives get dissolved. To remain free from all obstacles keep the divine company of learned, pure and competent persons. In the condition of adherence we should try to continuously divert our mental vision towards exclusive concentration on one entity. In case of confusions, we should, when obstacles come, understand the temporariness of destructable articles and move forward patiently towards attaining infinite bliss using renunciation etc.

When passion is an obstacle we should undertake auspicious determination and think of attachments, etc., that take the *Chitta* outward and make the aim unreachable and are hinderance in attaining the Supreme Spirit. Therefore, these should be discarded courageously. Being alert toward oneself, it is also essential to be cautions about entire reactions and then fixing oneself into divine experience. Keep awareness of such a divine state.

The experiences of the *Sadhak* encourage him. The experiences of oneself inspire oneself. The experiences are never out of sight, invisible, they remain always within the range. The object which is not the whole may appear to be certainly invisible sometime. The objects coming into the vision and experience of organs of sense are always out of sight. The attachment of *Chitta* with invisible object is invisible. But the experience of the 'Whole' under all times, circumstances and conditions is not invisible. *The Sadhak* must remain moving forward continoulsy in his *Sadhana*. The obstacles vanish by themselves with the experience of divinity. Therefore for the awareness of the 'Self' the *Sadhak* must remain rational and adequately conscious.

INTENTNESS

The doors of your hearts can be opened very easily with small keys like 'thankful', 'expressing gratitude with pleasant addressal'; meaning thereby that one should express his/her intent humbly, pleasantly, gracefully, honestly, sincerely, uprightly with humility and simplicity. To be simple, humble and graceful, are the arrangements of a person's character. There can be no other virtue for a person to be characterised as a great personality. Both Eastern and Western philosophers and learned persons have acknowledged and voiced the fact with a free, liberated, open and emancipated mind: '*Vidya Dadati Vinyam, Vinayadayati Pattratam*' i.e. 'Knowledge leads to humbleness and simplicity and humbleness/simplicity leads to worthiness.' Therefore, humbleness is the lone solid foundation of all the virtues of human beings and elements of humanity.

Goswami Tulsidas ji has described that knowledge is the root of humility. He has further gone beyond this virtue by expressing: 'It is because of its littleness (levity), that the ant is able to take along the crystal of sugar; whereas the elephant carries dust on his head'. In the context of simplicity, humankind feels peace within and renders peace to others as well, in behaviour. Humility is the off-spring of egolessness.

It means one must raise him-self through him-self and not fall down. 'Self' is the friend of 'Self' and also 'Self' is the enemy of 'Self'. Therefore, if one is righteous by his 'Self', he becomes pre-eminent. A benevolent person is humble, simple and a person of strong character.

Just as trees bend with the weight of fruits, gentle persons become most humble on getting plenty. God always helps and guides those who are humble and simple. Hailps has written-'Humility is the sure-shot medicine for most of the heart-felt troubles of humankind'. Ego is the darkness of night; humility and simplicity is the brightness of the day light. In the moments of humbleness and simplicity we are very close to greatness. Virtues and knowledge are like gold. But if we do not rub them to shine regularly, they will lose their beauty. It means that if we possess gold-like highly priced knowledge, then humility adds fragrance and brilliance to it. It is our duty to be humble and respectful with elders. It is etiquette (good manners) to be humble with equals. Being humble with youngers, acts as a protector and security. Ego makes a person a demon. Humility, (exactly opposite to this) simplicity, humanity takes a person towards godliness. Therefore, humility is the first and the last step of discriminating power (*vivek*) to understand what is right and wrong, real and unreal. Thus having good manners is the ultimate flower and climax of best conduct. In the society, therefore, the foremost expectation has been for good conduct, good manners and humility; and only thereafter comes education (knowledge) and virtues. Shashtras (spiritual scriptures) say: to the hands of those who hold the sword of forgiveness, no one can do any harm. When there is no expectation from any one, where is the sorrow and grief? Expectation from the world means making one self-dependent.

Those who have attained a state of balanced mind have won over the worldly matters. It means that during favourable-unfavourable situations the feeling of happiness-sorrow does not affect the state of a balanced mind. Just think about the life we live; we will come to know about the ups and downs faced many times. Humankind has laughed and many times he has cried. Humankind often becomes unsteady and fickle while moving along the worldly matters and therefore cannot peacefully find any resting place where he can relax for some time and release his stress and tiredness. The support that he takes after getting fed-up with the ever changing state of mind, is also in turmoil and is flowing in the same direction and motion. With the worldly upheavels, disturbences and beatings, the organs of sense get distracted and perplexed, the mind becomes anxious and afflicted and the intellect becomes dull; because the organs of sense start searching happiness and joy in worldly things. As a result, the situation takes an opposite turn and in unfavourable conditions uproar of grief/lamenation takes place. The intellect is unable to take any decision in such times, the mind fails to achieve success. In such a situation, seeing this phenomenal world as a witness and adopting humility as duty, one should surrender to a spiritual master, saint, shashtra, attaching himself to God; success is bound to come. We have not to spend anything in doing so; there is no expenditure involved. It is such a useful treasure that grows and grows day by day. God may forgive sins but there is no forgiving for notoriety. That is to say that one has to be humble and disciplined to attain final beatitude. It is a must. In humbleness and discipline there is neither fear nor ego. Good manners make humankind humane. Humility and endurance or forbearance are the two names of the same virture, i.e. one who is humble is bound to be patient naturally. When humankind is unified with respect to mind, speech and body, only then he can be successful in his mental resolve. The mental resolve should come into practice in one's speech and actions, performance of activities through body. Only under such conditions the mental resolve will never fail. By determination and thought process one can even control his anger. There should not be any worry in *Chitta* (mind, intellect and ego). This is what silence is. In this way humankind can become great.

God loves the human kind who is living in perfect equanimity with the opposites like, fame-defame, winter-summer, joy-sorrow, friend-enemy and always remembers Him and has little attachment with worldly things including the place where he lives.

SELF-DIRECTIVE

The mind of humankind is a store-house of many powers, abilities, energy, strength, prowess. These powers develop in accordance with the emotions of the mind. The self-determination becomes the cause of self-directive. This self-directive takes a person towards his determination and develops his abilities and strengths accordingly. In the state of ignorance any determination becomes valueless and useless. The more we go for introspection of the 'Self' to get directive knowledge, the stronger is our determination. Therefore one should repeatedly do introspection about the 'Self'.

The electronic energy is so strong that it cannot be broken. This energy is so strong that its misuse can be destructive but by its useful application, humankind can reach the highest peak of spirituality. However, currently this energy is being applied for a negative thought process. The human body is made of numerous atoms (electrons, protons).

How much energy is centered in atoms? is difficult to know. A humankind is not just a body; he is a live entity. He has been bestowed upon with the power to act, to control one-self and to know the 'Self'. These powers are absent in grossly non-living entities, because non-living entities neither possess any knowlege about the 'Self' nor they are dynamic. A living atom may be dynamic but does not possess the ability and power of self-control. Only the living atom of the human body has the ability to act, to control one-self and also to possess knowledge (*pragya, Gyan*). It is the center of energy and power. Not to know about one's 'Self', makes the humankind pitiable. In the absence of self-knowledge, the thought of what is out there sneaks into his mind and establishes a place which consequently, wise is wrong.

It is just like the state when a piece of rope lying on the way is understood to be a snake, in delusion and misapprehension; and in fear the person takes another path and gets lost in the woods of worldly life.

Until and unless one is capable of creating his path of life based on the light of knowledge, showered with the blessings of God through spiritual discourses of learned persons who have experienced the existence, he is bound to live in dellusion and can never find the Truth. Humankind is ignorant about his-self, about his powers, strength and energy; and due to ignorance, seeing a snake in the rope, under dellusion, has attained

'*Jiva Bhava*' (When bound in fetters, the Soul is the '*Jiva*', when released from them, the same thing is Shiv). Thus, looking for the everlasting '*Ananda*' (bliss) in the outer worldly pleasures, the Soul attains '*Jiva bhava*'. Such an effort is just hopeless and the one who is distracted from the main object of human life is bound to fall into misfortune. Humankind is a live atom. The atom itself is not capable of knowing its own strength nor of illuminating by itself. To do so, an aware (*chaitanya anu*) atom is required. The '*Chaitanya Anu*' knows self-strength and can transform itself, as per its own will and determination, into any form. The highest effort of humankind is 'Self-knowledge'. It is novel in itself. If the *Sadhak* (seeker) rises above joy-sorrow, he is sure to attain the blissful state. (*Sukh-dukh same krattva*). In joyful state, humankind exhibits concurrence, whereas in the state of sorrow, he gets distrubed, confused, perturbed and perplexed. This is the opportunity for introspection and to look at the 'Self'. Similarly the sense of liking and disliking takes the form of sorrow and joy in separated '*Jivas*'. A person disurbed by the agony of sorrow, feels joy as soon as the misery disappears. It is always so that after sorrow, joy is bound to come and after joy, sorrow is bound to come. Nobody remains miserable althrough, nor joyful for ever. One who wants to remain always happy must relinquish both sorrow and joy. It means that one should accept happily both sorrow and joy, as prosperity and adversity both are changeable.

The 'Sadhak' therefore must act according to resource oriented intellect. That is spiritual intelligence, the object of which is to know the ultimate reality (the Truth), the God. Such an objective leads to duty oriented actions. It is seen that even duty oriented actions cannot be performed efficiently. Only in the absence of attachment, selfishness and ulterior motives, duty oriented actions can be fruitful. Under such a state of mind one will never feel shortage of resources. He will never be deprived of resources. The Soul (*Jivataman*) is immortal. The actions and their results are subject to birth and death cycle. There has been no relation between immortal entity and the entities that are subject to give birth and death. Obviously there can be no relationship. It is just like a mirage. Therefore, considering what belongs to worldly matter must be left as worldly matter, leads to dissolution of the relationship between immortal Soul and perishable matter. Soul and body are two different entities. The former is immortal and the latter is mortal. The link with mortal matter is broken down by selfless action and this removes the ignorance. The actions not performed for selfish motives do not affect the 'Sadhak' (the seeker of the Truth). The 'Sadhak' thinks that even ego is not mine, it is the work of nature; therefore it does not affect him. The results of past actions do come as events in life, but considering that they are not related to 'Self' in Reality, the sorrow and joy have no effect on mind. A state of equanimity is attained.

JIVA' SALVATION

Whether it is animal-power, manly power, demon-power or Deva-power, none can stand in front of God's power. The demon Mahishasur had enormous animal power, the Kauravas had tremendous manly power, Ravan had immeasurable demon-power and *Indra* Deva and other Devas always possessed great power; but they all were defeated by God's power. The demon Mahishasur was killed by God in the form of Durgamata, Ravan was killed by God Sri Rama, Kaurvas were killed by Lord Krishna dependent—Pandavas. From the brilliance and power of Lord Krishna, *Indra* Deva had to accept defeat. Lord Krishna opposed *Indra Yagya* in 'Govardhan Hill', and settled the inhabitants of Brindavan, the 'Gopas'. Lord Krishna relieved all the inhabitants of 'Braj' from the terror of *Indra* Deva by lifting the 'Govardhan Hill' on his little finger's tip, when he was only a seven years old child. To do this impossible task, Lord Krishna used *Yog-Maya* power (*Krishnyoganubhavam*).

Having seen this supernatural power of Lord Krishna, the minds of 'Gopas' got bewildered. Supernatural power means the Eternal Power, the Divine Power, the Spiritual Power. 'Puran' literature has used several words for this supernatural spiritual power, e.g. *Yog-Maya*, Brilliance, Divine, Supreme, Omnipotent, Omnipresent. There are many such instances in the life of Lord Krishna, where He, with the help of powers of *Yog-Maya*, showed events full of miracles.

Yogeshwara Lord Krishna, as full incarnation of God (Vishnu), created events full of miracles with the use of *Yog*-power. 'Srimad Bhagvatam' and 'Gargsanghita' described the four stages of life of Lord Krishna : the childhood, the boyhood, the young lad and the youth. These scriptures also describe his childhood plays (*Leela*), e.g. showing his Universal Form, the Universe in his mouth, lifting of 'Govardhan Hill' on the tip of his little finger, removal of serpent 'Kalia' from Yamuna river, etc. These supernatural acts show the attributes of spiritual powers. While reciting Srimad Bhavad Gita, Lord Krishna is in the form of a young lad. This has also been confirmed by Goswami ji. Thus, most of the actions performed by Lord Krishna belong to childhood/boyhood stage and the stage of young lad and youth. All these are described in 'Dasham Skand' of 'Srimad Bhagvatam'.

Once, 'Brahma' willed to have a glimpse of the charmful greatness of Lord Krishna. Lord Krishna was busy in enjoying food with his boyhood friends; and the calves moved away in the deep forest for grazing. not seeing the calves, Lord Krishna went to search them. In the meantime, finding it as an appropriate moment, 'Brahma' removed the calves and hid them in hill caves. Lord Krishna understood the move of 'Brahma' and produced same number of calves to please Brahma and mothers of calves and his friends. This demonstrated lord Krishna's unbelievable miracle through his *Yog-Maya*.

From this it could be understood that without five elements, without actions of '*Jiva*' (live body) and without the name of emodiment of innerself, the omnipresent *Atma*n (Brahman) manifested, Himself in various forms to tell that He is omnipotent and omnipresent, the Reality. It also shows that for creation of any five element product, actor, reactor, *Jiva*, action, Brahman does not require anything. Brahman himself is manifested in the entire creation that we see. Rishi Durvasa was astonished to see Lord Krishna returning with his friends and this created a doubt in his mind about lord Krishna's identity as incarnation of Brhaman. Lord Krishna understood the state of mind of Rishi Durvasa and stood by the side of the Rishi. While Lord Krishna laughed, Durvasha Rishi entered into the stomach of Lord Krishna through the mouth. There the Rishi saw several universes, where the Rishi did his Spiritual practice (*Tapasya*) in several

Lokas, enjoyed the age of Brahman and then saw lord Krishna with *Gopas*, *Gopis* and cows. When he perceived such a view, Lord Kishna again laughed. With the second laugh of Lord Krishna, Rish Durvasha came out from Lord Krishna 's mouth. Then he saw Lord Krishna playing on the shore of Kalindi. This made him understand and know that Lord Krishna himself is omnipresent. Lord Krishna protected *Gopas, Gopis*, Cows calves by a fierce and powerful forest conflagration. Lord Krishna's *Yogmaya* was his main instrument in this eventful episode.

Lord Krishna created a joyful winter night by his *Yogmaya* for *Rasleela* (play) that lasted for six months.

Besides this, filing up the basket of a lady fruit vendor with most precious jewels indicates his omnipotence. Lord Krishna brought Nandji from *Varun-lok*. Hearing the narration about Varundeva from Nandji the hearts of Brijwasis became inquisitive to see Lord Krishna's own *Gaolok* and instantly Lord Krishna showed them his *Gaolok* which is beyond *Tamas*. *Gopas* having seen the Brahman Lok got the real *Anand* (Bliss). Likewise showing Rishi Durvasha to *Gopis* on the other shore of Yamuna through his *Yog Maya* showing Himself as Vishnu (Brahman) to Akrur Ji in Yamuna's water, in the war with demon Jarasang increasing his army by his *Yog* power, establishing all Yadavas in His Dwarika by Yogpower indicates that Lord Krishna (Brhaman) is omnipotent, omnipresent and omniscient.

When God comes in form for the uplift of his creation in the world, God says :

Even if there is no action, no expectation of action or no necessity of action, God continues to work for the benefit of his creation and there is no stopping in His action. Lord Krishna spent every moment in His *Leela* in performing creations supernaturally.

POWER OF RIGHT UNDERSTANDING THE TRUTH

The feeling and inner knowledge of the existence of God comes to us when we go beyond the outer knowledge of our sensual organs and piercing the fear of mind and intellect. Among the instruments of this knowledge; the first instrument is purity of intellect. Man's intellect is of dual nature blended or dependent on others and pure self-dependent. The action of intellect that lies within the circumference of the expereinces of sensual organs is blended or dependent on others. It takes this principle as true, and makes efforts to utilize in the same manner under the influence of outer knowledge of object and interrelations as perceived by sensual organs. Contrary to this, pure work of the intellect comes at the time when it does not work under the influence of the knowledge coming from sensual organs but works under the experiences touched through the power of its innerself, tries to stabilise such irreversible innerself universal thoughts, that are not bound by external features of objects; meaning thereby it is attached to the existence which is beyond the external form of the objects. The intellect bounded by external form of objects can immediately recognise the object by seeing and examining it. But the pure intellect uses its experiences just for the cause and before taking decision leaves that experience far behind and so much away and behind that the inner outcome may be entirely different or opposite from the outcome judged by the experiences based on sensual organs. This kind of the business of the intellect is always justified and not to be shunned; the reason being, that the common experience of humankind is just a fraction of the events happening in the world and the universe and for this little fraction, the instruments and the reason used are defective by nature; and therefore the outcome is not right. Cleaning the defects of the mind, directed by organs of sense, by intellect, is a special power that has been bestowed upon humankind by the grace of God. That is why humankind is considered best among all other living creatures. Complete utilization of the intellect, takes out humankind from the circumference of physical knowledge and leads him to the entry into spiritual knowledge. Spiritual knowledge satisfies our pure intellect though, because purity of intellect exists on the ground of spiritual knowledge and our nature looks at objects, with our two eyes, in two forms : one is emotion or feeling and the other is materialistic aspect. Therefore, any principle remains incomplete and false for our innate nature till it becomes a subject of our experience. To get the knowledge of material object, there must be another act that can satisfy our common nature and such an act is achievable by increasing the performance of our mind in this material world. The experiences gained by mental activities, like the knowledge attained by intellect work with duality: (i) blended or dependent on others and (ii) pure or self-dependent. Its blended action is, when our conscience explores to know the objects of outer world and pure/self-dependent work is, when inner faculty explores to know the 'Self' — innate nature. In the former case a person is dependent on organs of sense and whatever knowledge is gathered is based on the knowledge supplied by organs of sense. In the latter case the knowledge gained is through the work of inner-self and it works within and in this manner one gets the exactly true knowledge about the objects encountered. Thus, we know about the states of our mind as well as knowledge about anger etc., because we ourselves become the same. In fact the knowledge gained by experience is real knowledge coming as a result of our connectivity. But its reality remains hidden, because we have separated ourselves from the other world on account of our individual nature of separatism. We have taken ourselves as the knower and object of concern. That is why we have to prepare ourselves for such resources and actions which can connect us to the Truth or Reality from which we have dissociated ourselves. It means that our present worldly bondages are not essential for us. For inner-self it is possible and practical and it will be but natural that the inner-self must free itself from the nature of coming into the influence of the perishable worldly objects and achieve the ability and capability for inner absorption of the organs of sense without taking their help. Same results, as expressed above, are obtained in experiments of sleep dominion and other similar experiments on chain of mental activities. The awakened state of awareness in destined and limited by the coordination and harmony between the inner-self coming as a result of development of life process and the matter (sensuality). That is why the knowledge obtained about the inner-self awakened state of awareness cannot be compared with common state of awareness based on organs of sense. Therefore, to achieve the knowledge based on inner-self, the mind is to be brought under a kind of state of sleep. In this way the real inner-self gets free and it comes into its real form (innate form). Thus the inner-self accepts itself alone as always omnipresent, free sense and leaves the blended and dependent path for knowing the controller of senses. The inner-self independently and freely becomes competent to do work with purity. It becomes self-dependent. It is not impossible to strengthen the mind using such an expansion-resource; but in our wake-up state it is some what difficult. When senses like mind and inner-self start doing self-dependent and pure action, then the other senses besides the common ones, can also be developed. But even with these powers our goal remains, unaccomplished. The inner-self is still unable to experience the truths that are beyond the comprehension of organs of sense, nonetheless that are perceptible by intellect. The true form of the matter is beyond perceptibility of senses. However, in the structure of world's life system there is such an in-built order as to whenever there is intellect perceptible *Tattva* (innate nature/Soul) there, within the multitude acts connected with intellect, do exist the means to know or experience that *Tattva* (Soul). One of the means that exists in our inner-self through which we are able to know about our existence (the Brhaman, the Soul, the God.), is the special attribute of knowledge gained by that connectivity. The knowledge as to what is inside in our inner-self, depends to a greater or lesser extent, upon conscious knowledge. In common terms and language it can be said that the knowledge about permeable (able to be the knowledge of pervaded) is within the knowledge of all pervasive.

Therefore if we expand the power of our mental self-experience beyond ourselves towards experiencing externally existing authority-power /sovereignty of Soul or Brahman, then the truth of power of all pervading Brahman and the Soul, as described in Upanishad, can be the subject of our experience. The Indian philosophy is established and founded as an institution on the basis of practicability and accessibility of such experiences. Using this, as a knowledge of Soul, Indian philosophy has researched on Existence (knowledge of universe). But in this very philosophy (Vedanta), the experiences of mind and intellectual thoughts have been considered only as reflection lying connected with the inner-self-it is not self proven *Tattva* (Oneness of Brahman). To experience the oneness of Brhaman we have to go beyond mind and intellect. In the consciousness of our wakeful state of intellect, the intellect works as intermediary between the dullest consciousness and the ever conscious internal consciousness. In the dull consciousness, the knowledge of consciousness is located in *Karma* (action). Cause-action is the essence of life. The special and distinctive work of dull consciousness is life, whereas the distinctive work of ever conscious eternal consciousness is light. In the ever conscious eternal consciousness *Karma* (actions) re-enters into light and here no knowledge is located under it. Here only the 'Self' resides in ever conscious eternal consciousness.

The inner wisdom is that wisdom which is equally present in both. The base of inner wisdom is knowable relationship between knower and known. This commonality in both sides is that state of self-proof, where the knower and known, as a result of knowledge, become one. But in dull consciousness, there is suitable exposition of inner-knowledge through *Karma* (action). Oneness of knowledge or true knowledge is, to a greater or lesser extent, always hidden in *Karma* (action). Contrary to this, in ever conscious eternal consciousness, light being *Dharma* and *Tattva* (Brahman), the oneness in inner-knowledge and knowledge comes out as Ultimate Reality and consequently *Karma* (action), according to one's competence. Being the original *Tattva*, Brahman does not hide his identity. In between both the states the intellect and mind act as intermediary, in such a way that the Soul gets ready to come to her original state (peace, love, happiness, bliss) by freeing the knowledge from the bondage of *Karma* (action). When mind's spiritual knowledge or knowledge of 'Self' goes in permeable and all pervading (both in the self-Soul and universal Soul)and appears as self-illuminating light, then the intellect also gets transformed into illuminated inner knowledge.

This is the supreme state of our knowledge. In this state of knoweldge our inner-self reaches the highest knowledge and attains wholeness.

TRUTH IS SHIV; SHIV IS BEAUTIFUL

S hiv and *Shakti* are inseparable from each other like sun and light, fire and its heat and milk and its whiteness. Worshipping Shiv is to worship *Shakti* and worshipping *Shakti* is to worship Shiv. They are two forms of *Param Tattva* (Brahman, Soul, Everlasting Eternal Existence). Shiv is the Soul *Tattva* and *Shakti* is the resultant. The foundation and governing of the exposition of *Shakti* in various scenes in numerous unique forms in the world is Shiv. Shiv is inperceptible, unseen, omnipresent, changeless Soul. *Shakti* is the establishment of power of heart, and name and form. *Shakti*, on the endless peaceful and profound region of chest of Shiv, taking the form of numerous universe is always dancing, performing three fold — *Leela* (play) relating to the world continuance and destruction. In the *Vaaksukta, Parambha* (*Shakti*) has shown her divine intent herself. The galaxies of universe, since beginning, are only in glory of the feet of the Supreme '*Etavansya mahima*' and three times more than this, it is in the '*Dyulok*' (space beyond sky) '*Par Odiva Per Ena Prathivya*'; meaning thereby the space beyond both earth and sky; far beyond. Aloneness, neutral, Soul and ever-new consciousness.

There is no end of intermediate or secondary powers of the supreme power (*Shakti*), rejoicing power, multitute group power, wisdom power, desire power, action power, will power.

Brahmsutra tells that the purpose of this creation is just the *Leela* (play). There is no other purpose, besides *Leela* (play). '*Lokvaktuleela Kayualayam*'. For organising *Leela* the supreme power uses two types of *Shakti*, collective *Shakti* and *Maya Shakti* (illusive power). Rigveda Radhopanishad describes that this collective *Shakti* in three way exposition tranforms herself into *Leela*'s useful dwelling (Paradise) aseatic seat, sleeping bed, clothes, ornaments etc. She becomes friend, service person, God's companion. God himself says that He incarnates with the support of collective *Shakti* (power), means that use of collective *Shakti* is essential in creating and organising *Maya* (illusion, supernatural power). '*Prakrati swamdhishthaya sambhavabhyatama mayaya*.' It is natural that the accomplishment of most excellent *Shakti* is more important than Brahman (the creator). *Maya Shakti* (illusive power) also contains dellusive power (attachment). A believer of individuality of Soul, tries to prove the conscious live world as the pleasure of illusive power attached to individual Soul, illustrating individual Soul – World – God as form of dreamy state created for self-pleasure.

Brahman dependent *Maya Shakti* (illusive power) is extraordinary distingusishing characteristic, pure intellegence, Supreme Being and extra-ordinary bliss. Brahman dependent visible world power is extraordinary in comparison to Brhaman, in a manner like the Brahman characterised burning power is extraordinary than Brahman.

Brahman is *Tattva* (Everlasting External Existence) and *Maya* is *Nistattva* (everchanging appearances). Despite this, the everchanging appearance of *Maya* remains covered due to imitation of Brahman. When characteristic Brahman, using subtle intellegence, is separated from the entire body (pervaded by the supreme being), then the changing character of that thing appears (becomes evident). Such type of power, to the eyes of worldly persons, appears to be real, to the eyes of logicians it is inevitability and in view of listener it is worthless.

The basic characteristic of untruth and falsehood is the same. The thing that is not resplendent appears to be evident and the thing that is not evident appears to non-resplendent, that is untruth. Non-existence is the original nature of both (untruth and falsehood); resplendence or non resplendence is only intermediate difference. *Shakti* and Her works are considered coverage of matter – *Tattva* and at the same time expressive.

There are two forms of *Shakti* : (i) Inner and (ii) Outer.

Just as Brahman dependent visible world is accepted as outer world; that is dull consciousness; collective ever blissful *Shakti* is inner *Shakti* and ever conscious consciousness. The Truth being oneness, *Chitta* getting illuminated, the bliss is ever joyful and accounts for the *Shakti* that provides a state of being ever blissful.

According to *'Shevatashwatropanishad'* knowledge, strength and action *Shakti* are the peculiarty of Brahman *Shakti*. *'Bhavnopanishad'* also gives an account of knowledge, desire and action *Shakti*. Just as in livng creatures, aquired knowledge of the world, spiritual or mental knowledge and breathing/living knowledge, respectively, are principal action *Shakti*. Similarly God possesses all the three kinds of *Shakti*. Desire *Shakti* is *Yog Shakti* of God and is located in south portion as particular mark on the breast of lord Vishnu/Krishna.

The form of *'Yog Shakti'*, action *Shakti* is spiritual. Enjoyment of pleasures of senses *Shakti* is physical, and *Vir Shakti* is caused by fate. Knowledge *Shakti* is manifestation and *Shakti* covering *Shakti* of *Chitta* (mind, intellect, ego). Will power is the manifestation *Shakti* and covering *Shakti* of bliss (*Anand*). Action *Shakti* is the manifestation *Shakti* and covering *Shakti* of the Truth. This way in *Sat-Chitta-Anand*, there is end of knowledge, action and will.

Birth and death, beginning and end of the world is Shiv-*Shakti*. Motherly divine fire and

Savita-Savitri form proves the same. Assignment of various parts of the body to different deities which is accompanied by prayers and corresponding gesticulations for worshiping Shiv-*Shakti* has extraordinary importance. To be out of bondage and to be god-like, rishi-like and fully accomplished like, we should essentially take the support of entrustment; for *Shakti*-protection requires meditation of *Shakti*. In accomplishment of *Mantra*, Rishi, God, will, source, power and application have extraordinary importance, but all this knowledge is kind and beneficial only when it is directly coming from the mouth of *Guru* (the spiritual master, representative of Brahma, Vishnu and Shiv). By great sacrificial acts, placing part of body by sacrificial act, by purification of earth and purification of evil and by following religious rituals of one's own caste, *Shiv Shakti Bhava* springs out. This is the only path of supreme welfare, prosperity, good fortune, virtuous/auspicious action.

INNER JOURNEY

B rahman nectar is supernatural, trascendental and rare. In the world matter, there is no such supernaturality. In the world, whenever there is a little bit experience of joy that is not even a fraction of Brahman bliss. The worldly joy is just a shadow. Even this shadow is, only sometimes, experienced only by a few. It is not always experienced, nor everywhere. This shadow is also of Brahman nectar. It is the form of all of us but attachment with body has covered it. One who renunciates attachment with body, he remains everywhere always drenched entirely with this nectar, and other juices become meaningless and tasteless. He feels always satisfied and contented, considers it supreme and even in greatest misery experiences the same fulfilment. He is never disturbed in inconvenience and difficulty. He is stable, firm, angerless and durable/imperishable. There is Brahman everywhere in this ever changing world, yet one has to rennunciate the proud of body to attain knowledge of Brahman. In the disguise of body proud it is not possible to know and experience Brahman. As soon as body proud vanishes, knowledge of Brahman reveals, and sorrow, attachment, fear go away.

We can experience the presence of God, in this ever changing world. The world is not different from God. Therefore, despite the existence of the world we can experience and get the knowledge of the presence of God, just as despite the pitcher being there, it is understandable to know the soil/clay. One who does actions in the love of God in his several births, his inner-self gets purified. Due to purified inner-self, one renunciates the body and the falseness related to body, attachment with perishable matter; and takes shelter in God. It is said that a learned person after testing peoples act attains renunciation, because actionlessness cannot be known by activities. Thinking like this, taking a completely dry piece of twig one should approach to a learned spiritual master (*Shrotriya Brhamanist Guru*) to get the knowledge of the everlasting *Tattva* (the Truth, the Reality). One who is truly inquisitive to know the Supreme, Self knowledge, it is essential for him to the have the real knowledge of body element; '*Sharirmadhyam Khalu Dharmasadhanam*', is a profound truth. *Jiva* (Soul), from times immemorial is trapped into the cluthces of the world as a result of unutterable power, and therefore knowledge of the 'Self' is attainable and expressive only with the support of the body. Actually *Jiva* has forgotten his-self and his pure consciousness has become dull, tarnished, vicious and wicked. And due to indecisiveness it is appearing as action-cause-effect. Body is not a permanent thing; it is impermanent and perish. Despite thinking this way and wishing to oneself away from the thought of being body, due to the blow of natural power *Jiva*'s body consciousness feeling, common person thinks by the body (in the language of scriptures) that it is nothing but gross body; and in fact there is no other thing for the development of body-*Tattva*.

When physical atomic mass gets concentrated at a special place and takes the shape of a point. Whether it is through combination of ovum and semen or otherwise, then that point is to be understood as seed, origin, source, (embroy, foetus). This body seed strengthens receiving raw material from outside and at fixed time takes form to come to perform work. The ovum-semen like blood and pure white combination point, either due to natural or artificial influence meet with each other in agitative state (state of sorrow) and light up in form of emproy. Until the humankind by following sequencial practice of celibacy, achieve state of firmness and ascent, state of his descent is obvious. Commonly, this is the state of humankind. In this state having not achieved control over desire, the semen movement is bound to be downward. But those who vow and practice celibacy and have control over passion, they have to calm down their desires by will power or skillful actions, in order to keep themselves away from the actions of gross creation. Until and unless the concept of particle state of seed is overruled, there is remote possibility of any kind of dynamic development. In absence of dynamism, the creation is like flower in sky. The desireless feelings of ascent is cultivational towards perfection; and therefore such persons do not have the passion and desire that natural men would possess. This type of creative desire is called artificial desire. Commonly the gross body works with help of strength and power. In the basics of setting gross body in motion, knowledge and action power are present. The senses of knowledge are the stream of knowledge power and senses of action are the stream of action power. Both the streams equally participate in inner-self. Senses, etc are, in fact, the special brilliance power of activeness of body. This brilliance called Ling body. This, despite being undivided appears as divided. It is permeated with the gross body through and through; just as fire exists in a piece of wood . . . but not visible, it is to be awakened by special actions.

INNATE STATE

'Parinamtap Samskar dukhaigurnvratti-virodhhachch dukhmeva sanavivekinah'

The result of materialistic joy is sorrow. In the states of joy there exists some relationship. Under the situations encountered in relative joy, the greater joyfullness of others create greater sorrow. As soon as the state of joy recedes, the memories of better joyful state makes one more miserable. It means that no one is devoid of states of the joy and sorrow. Even a happy person, due to grinding/friction of *Sattva, Rajas* and *Tamas* powers, gets distressed and afflicted by greed. But a judicious person with discriminating capability remains always in blissful state. Truth pervails in all occasions. In this creation only one effort of human kind is evident everywhere and that is attaining comfort and joy. And humankind is searching joy in untruth, thinking that money is the base of all joy and comfort, has been clearly stated. The majesty and grandeur of the world does not lie in money; it exists in minimum needs. Money lights up desires and sacrifice, renunciation provides satisfaction. The greatest truth of the world is death. It is immmpossible to escape from the clutches of death. One who understands this truth, he is wise.

In fact death is just like changing old clothes. Our greatest duty is to obtain real knowledge and to achieve it we must search for a *Sadguru* (spiritual master). In absence of *Sadguru* we go on committing mistakes and remain engrossed in worldly affairs and remain miserable.

It should be clearly understood that God is no different than the world, there is no difference in any matter/object, the difference that we see is an illusion. What has happened, what will happen and what is happening at present and what is not happening is all God. Due to our ignorance we have not been able and we are unable to recognise this truth. After getting such supreme knowledge, all illusions go away; all the things/objects become Godly and the attachment with changing matter is destroyed.

Lord Shiv has averred in clear words:

Ekam Gyanam Nityamadhyant Shunyam,
Nanyat Kinchad Vartate Vastu Satyam!
Yabhedosminnindriypadhan Vai,
Gyanasyayam Bhaste Nanayyathav!!

One everlasting, original-endless knowledge is the Truth. The knowledge is the foundation of *Shakti* (Strength/power), senses of knowledge and intellect. As a result of spiritual development the role of senses become limited. The senses of a common person can feel and see only the gross matter present in this world. Spiritual development awakes our divine senses. There is no hurdle in the movement of divine senses. The gap between *Desh* and *Kaal* (place and time) as well, amounts to nothing for divine senses. The intellect of humankind, tries to take decision on the basis of guess work. In the event of senses attaining divinity, the area of our vision being very expansive, even our guess work will present greater truth in comparison to what we guess in absence of divinity. In fact with spiritual development the ordinary argumentative intellect also calms down and is replaced by spiritual spring (energy). The real resolve comes up to know about any subject. Our knowledge starts getting real and determined. This transformational change in intellect slowly and slowly reaches to highest level. Earlier the mind was getting influenced by joy-sorrow or used to lose its natural state. As a result of spiritual development there occurs transcendental firmness. There remains no feeling as sorrow-joy. Equanimity comes easily, automatically. Keeping equanimity intact, needs no efforts.

It happenes due to the fact that consciousness gets firmly established at a higher level. When there is no pressure on mind, then the mind becomes intention free (void); this is the innate state of saints (state of trance — the mind successfully fixed upon ultimate being and with the senses completely restrained in final state of *Yog*). Mind or heart is the centre of emotions, joy — sorrow, attachment — haterd, sensuality — anger, love — service, sympathy, parental affection. Spiritual development also brings transformation in these attributes. Purification of mental store house, as a result of the appearance of *Tamsik* and *Rajsic* impulses is not possible. When *Sattavic Bhava* takes their place, sensuality and anger calms down. A smooth grudgeless empire of love, service, selflessness fills the heart. The vow power becomes determination. Vows always reach completion and the awakened Soul power purifies the body. The alien matter gets rejected. Therefore, self-development is the real spiritual development. This development is not one-sided, it is all through and through. This development:

> *Yatoabhyayudnisheyas Sidhhih Sah*
> *Dharmah* always complete the
> indications of above cited *Dharma*.

Sympathy, compassion, selflessness and service, should successfully come into action; it should not be just emotional. Sensuality and anger etc. continuously start get going away. Increasing equanimity, happiness and peace rise in the mind. Resolves should be powerful. Victory over petty matters. All these are externally evident features and indicators of spiritual growth.

Spirituality is elixir-like mother form. Love is its heart. "Self" vigour/energy/enthusiasm is its mind. Uninterrupted action power is its resolve. Truth and discipline are its strong legs, service and self-sacrifice are its arms, the blood of equanimity continuously flows into its veins and artries. People's benefit and welfare are its fellow companions. Innate fragrance of bliss continuously flows. The Ultimate Enlightenment comes by strong relationship with such attributes.

LORD SHIV

'Brahmoti Parmatameti bhagvaniti shabdyate'

According to the Principle of *Sanatan Dharma*, Brahman, Supreme Soul and God are one and the same. That one everlasting external existence is being worshiped by very many names-forms and adoration traditions. In worship, any Godly form can be made as aim, but in such case worship has been considered as the main aspect. One who worships his Idol with fullest adoration and prayers, he is rewarded accordingly. By God's grace only the humankind has been betowed upon the great opportunity to worshipping God; *'Tassam me paurushi priya'*: Because of this, praying God is essential tool and resource to achieve happiness and pleasure in this world and also in the world beyond this world. The prime aim of human life is to experience 'Self' (Soul, the Brahman, God, the Truth, EEE

or whatever we call). Rule of good conduct/
behaviour, cleanliness, etc. are to be adhered
to. In worhipping, purification of these five;
place, time, doer, matter and *Mantra*, is essential.
Since God's creation is governed by three Gunas
(*Sattva, Rajas* and *Tamas*), every human being is
different with regard to his nature, preference and
temperament. Therefore it is said : '*Ekam Sad Vipra
Bahudha Vadanti*'. Only one Brhaman is in many
forms and in universal form. The God (Brhaman)
is omnipresent, omnipotent and omniscient. He
is subtler than subtle, void of cause and effect.
The supreme Soul (Brhaman) is the creator of
this ever changing world, ever lasting eternal
existence and ever dynamic form is His greatest
godliness. Complete form of welfare, auispicious
and supremely peaceful, Lord Shiv is synonym
of auspiciousness of the entire world. Lord Shiv
is root place of all the rules and laws. There is no
other *Tattva* in equality to Lord Shiv in respect of
knowledge, force, desire and action power.

Lord Shiv being the root cause, basic
foundation, protector, saviour and everlasting of
all gods is known as MAHAMAHESHAWRA. He
himself has no cause and base.

Lord Shiv is worship God of all gods, master
of all masters, everlasting, having no beginning
and end, unborn, beyond wakeful, deamy and
sleep states, fully illuminated in *Turiyavastha* (the
fourth state of Soul in which it becomes one with
Brhaman or Supreme spirit); meaning thereby that
He is EEE. Lord Shiv gets easily pleased and that is
why gifts, *Dharma*, money, desire/wish, salvation,

knowledge—science of life and anything. In Vedas and other sacred texts, Lord Shiv has been designated as form of pure knowledge. Just not gods alone but rishis, munis, gyanis, dhyanis, vidyadhar, asur, naag, kinnar, charan and human being etc. all by worshiping Lord Shiv, continously meditating upon him, praying and performing *Yagya* etc. obtain his blessings and kindness and attain quality of Shiv. The characteristics of Lord Shiv are extraordinarily—generous and full of compassion. He is supreme Idol of knowledge, renunciation and sainthood. The deadly poision produced during churning of ocean was swallowed by Lord Shiv, at the request of Lord Vishnu and by *Yog* power Lord Shiv absorbed it in His throat. It caused blueness to the throat and that is why, He is called Neelakanth. As Lord Shiv is holding the sacred river Ganga in his matted hair, He is known as Gangadhar. There are innumerous names of Lord Shiv His greatness, glory and grandeur is endless. He is the Supreme Lord, worshiped by all. He gave fame to several demons also (Mahish, Tripur, Ravan). On the other hand killed several demons : Gajasur, Bhasmasur, Tripurasur etc. and provided salvation. Due to the grace Lord Shiv Lokpals got proprietorship (head of a religious order) of North direction, headship of Yakshas. etc. In view of *Tattavic* vision, there is no difference between Lord Shiv and Lord Vishnu. (*Yatha Shivmayo Vishnurevam Vishnumayaha Shivah*) (Lord Vishnu, Lord of supernatural magical or wonderful power i.e. Lord of *Maya*), Ramapati (Lord Vishnu) and

Umapati (Lord Shiv), Mahadev, both are order of knowledge, religous austerity, eight-step *Yog* and divine majesty. These two Lords are incharge of the welfare of the world and director. They are one and the same Soul of each other and continuously worship each other and are enagaged in praying for resource of benevolence for each other. Purans say that Shiv and Vishnu are inner-self and heart of each other : *Shivasya hradiyam hradiyam Shiv'*. They are one and the same; there is no differnece *'Sarvam Shivamyam Jaga'*. Only Shiv is revealing and appearing in numerous different forms. All are Brahman and nothing else. Only Brahman. Due to ignorance and diverse intellect, under the influence of *Maya* (illusion), humankind thinks himself to be separate entity from God. Moving and immovable all are forms of Shiv. All are Shiv and Shiv is all. Learned persons who have experienced Brahman come to know Shiv-*Tattva* and get enlightened and become Shiv-like. The knowledge of Shiv-*Tattva* comes from Shiv worship. Shiv and *Shakti* are two forms of supreme *Tattva*. Shiv is Soul *Tattva* and *Shakti* is the resultant. Shiv is invisible, omnipresent changeless Soul. *Shakti* is visible, movable, expressed as name and form. *Shakti* dances on the endless peaceful and unfathamable breast of Shiv, taking the form of numerous universe. Inhere dance *Shakti*, does *Leela* (play) of creation and destruction.

TURMOIL OF MIND

When light kindles the '*Tamas*' (darkness) vanishes. As soon as light comes in the dark layers of darkness, the darkness starts disintegrating automatically. The darkness cannot stand in front of light, cannot face light because the presence of light destroys the existence of darkness. Now there is a question; in presence of light does the darkness really get destroyed? It exists; the darkness is there. Silently the darkness waits for the opportunity of letting the light to extinguish and then I can reappear; and it happens exactly like this. As soon as the light is extinguished, the linen of darkness again spreads over.

When the light of the Truth kindles in any corner of mind, the darkness of ignorance starts disappearing and the song and music of devotion for God starts. When the desire that is the call (quest) for seeking the Truth, shakes up the existence; then transformation in oneself starts taking place; catharsis starts taking place. In this state when the desire that is the quest for seeking the Truth becomes painful and the pain keenly looks for a solution; then the entire existence drenching itself in love for God give life to the possibilities of the seeker (*Sadhak*) of the Truth. Song and music of the Truth Revelation get generated in one's heart. Such moments and opportunities put oneself into a state of achievement beyond comprehension where only 'Self' exists and nothing else.

What a wonder, greatest wonder! The solution of pain is 'Self'. In the journey of 'Self' unfoldment, the solution starts coming nearer and nearer.

Solution provides satisfaction. When every corner of existence proceeds towards finding solution, then solution comes nearer and nearer. We commit mistakes when we get closer. The solution achieved disintegrates, knowledge about self disappears. Again the desire to seeking the Truth and realization of 'Self' awakens and again the strings of music of the Truth start resonance. Then again mistake and disappearance. Why the realization of 'Self' disappears and where it gets lost?

In the lack of awareness about the 'Self', the opportunity that knocked is lost. As we reach closer to shore, the possibility of getting drowned increases, why? Because the knowledge that we are close to the shore gives birth to laziness. Excessive awareness and knowledge about closeness of destination also hinders the set goal.

Let the pain, the desire in the quest of seeking the Truth deepen, crying increase. This deep pain and crying will invite your awareness towards

'Self' that is from outthere to inhere and your journey will move towards blissfulness. As soon as the attention concentrated in outside business takes its journey inwards, the awareness of the turmoil and chaos in the existence will make you deeply conscious about 'Self'.

In the lack of awareness, the flow of consciousness is outward. Even one moment of caution can astonish you with the beauty of 'Self'; but non alertness (casualness), unconsciousness and inactiveness of one moment can become misery of whole life. Awake from deep sleep. Existence is inviting you. Call — 'Self' call is constantly sounding in you. In this call your 'Self' is calling you. How long this hide and seek game will go on? In this call of 'Self' and in desire for seeking the Truth, your alertness is inviting your attention towards inexhaustible treasure of self esteem, self beauty, self popularity in the kingdom of 'Self'. Get up, wake up, be careful so that you can realize 'Self', your Soul.

The ambassadors of everlasting peace are waiting for you and the light (knowledge, wisdom), tremendous light is waiting to drench you with Divinity; ambassadors of Soul are calling, be the owner of your 'Self' and that is your goal.

Be alert! Soldiers of blind desires (sensual desires) are eagerly waiting for a state of your not being cautious.

Therefore in the state of burning desire to seeking the Truth, happiness and awareness try to experience 'Self' in between 'To be' and 'To becoming', peace is within you. *Om Shanti, Shanti, Shanti.*

INTROSPECTION – SELF EVALUATION AND PURIFICATION

The current state of affairs in the entire world, without any doubt, represents the fact that the materialistic developments do not convey the advancement in terms of peace, purity, unity, love and harmony. To-day on all sides the human existence is surrounded by materialistic influences. Under the great dependence of physical comforts man is giving prime importance to material applications for achieving happiness. This all is due to ignorance about reality and lack of awareness. The state of our Soul (*Jiva-tattva*) can be well assessed on the basis of how much importance we assign to materialistically sensual and phenomenal world. As much as you value the sensual world, to the same extent your value goes down. That is, it is inversely proportional.

The greater the vision of phenomenal world you have, the smaller you become. Your own identity will be of no consequence, because all assets and values of your life will get attached to this changing world. Your life looses its meaning all-too-easily. When your entire consciousness gets attached with outer world, when you start giving importance and value to the outer world out-there then you start devaluing your own self. When a person gets fully attached with any material thing, he loses his own identity as a human being.

Today the man is away from 'Self'. He is living a pitiable life being away from his own Self, from his everlasting existence. In a way he is living a dead life, because if one limits himself and his life to material world outthere, he is as good as dead to that extent. Under such a situation we are not fully alive. We got human life, a part of which got attached to material things excessively, that we think and consider separate from 'Self'. Our life is not meant to go downward. Its every moment is a gifted opportunity to achieve Divinity and godliness. Therefore, it is invaluable and priceless. Every moment of life is to be devoted to those practices that are made available to us by God for leading a meaningful and purposeful life. Therefore, a *Sadhak* (seeker) should thoughtfully and faithfully decide that every material thing in this world is perishable. Ignorantly men consider them as their own possessions, whereas they are not. Ignorantly accepted possessive associations one day get dissociated. As long as man considers these perishable and impermanent things of comfort, he is not able to accept fully his everlasting relationship with God, which is ceaseless love. Do not get attached to any object, matter or situation. Whatever is available, use it usefully. Proper utilization of what is available and no expectation of that which is not available leads to dissolution of attachment automatically. Dissolution of attachment automatically removes envy and jealousy. The retardation of attachment and envy brings retardation in unwanted sensualities. Thereafter, uncalled for desires do not rise. This is the solution that takes one towards happiness, peace, purity and love for humanity.

In this ever-changing life wherever man is experiencing reality and love, it is manily due to relationship between duality and non-duality (*Bhedbhava* and *Abhedbhava*). If the distinction between duality and non-duality is removed, then the identity and grossness is transformed into 'Awareness of 'Self''; meaning thereby establishing union with God. In such a state attachement is converted into renunciation and enjoyment into 'Yoga' (unification) i.e., dissolution of *Chitta* and *Vratti*. However, it is not possible without purity of mind, body, *Pran* and psyche. To achieve the goal, if a man does not apply easily available resources and depends upon other things, he cannot purify his mind, body, *Pran* and psyche; and under such a situation the life remains away from the Ultimate Reality (the Truth).

What appears to be the source of joy and happiness is actually the cause of sorrow when seen with eye of wisdom. What is pleasing in the beginning is the cause of sorrow when experienced through practicing 'Ashtanga Yoga'. During Sadhana one may experience uneasiness and sorrow in the beginning but ultimately the result is permanent happiness. So one should not leave his Sadhana in-between. Worldly enjoyments have always resulted in misery. The materials that we are enjoying as a pleasure, they are certainly going to be cause of unhappiness in the event of their non-availability. It will become a miserable case of helplessness. A true seeker of the Truth through his wisdom can realize that renunciation is indeed essential. As long as there is a feeling of pleasure in material things, there is no possibility of renunciation. In absence of renunciation, books, pilgrimage, spiritual discourses and scriptures cannot provide real happiness (permanent happiness). One must have full faith in the words of the Spiritiual Master (Guru), as to what is real and what is unreal. With the Divine grace of Guru, the Sadhak in quest of the Truth experiences the Ultimate Reality. Until and unless there is detachment from enjoyments and pleasures derived from material things, the Sadhak would not get real blissfulness. The understanding that the body is perishable and temporary reduces the attachment. The real Sadhak of the Truth truthful disciples always try to keep themselves away from mean desires. They continuously remain engrossed in thinking of indestructible Ultimate Reality (Everlasting Tattva), leaving behind perishable matter/object;

and aspire for that ultimate bliss which provides permanent happiness.

Worldly pleasures are limited temporary and deceptive. Favorable situations, objects and materials may provide pleasure; and if conditions become unfavorable they cause misery. But in this phenomenal world everything, every situation is changing; sometimes things are favorable and sometimes unfavorable. It is not possible for a man to have favorable conditions always. Favorable or unfavorable are relative perceptions. It is because of the attitude man feels miserable. Sensual joys/ pleasures and sorrows are both impermanent. The availability of those objects which provide pleasures and joys; their non-availability renders misery. There is nothing permanent with respect to sensual pleasures and comforts. Which is not permanent cannot provide permanent happiness. A person due to attachment to the things can enhance his comforts, but in fact permanent happiness is not there.

The thing that cannot provide permanent happiness, how can that be considered to be the cause of permanent happiness? It is our ignorance that we consider the worldly objects as a source of happiness. This ignorance can only be removed by the Divine grace of the Spiritual Master (*Guru*); because this ignorance is a symptom of illusive vision. The result of action can be countered by action, but the result of illusive vision due to ignorance cannot be countered by action. It can only be removed by wisdom (*Gyan*); just as to remove darkness light is necessary.

The plenty in worldly pleasures is not due to any action, it is due to ignorance. Therefore, it can only be removed by knowledge and understanding the falsehood of world and not by action. Action would help remove impure desires. With the Divine grace of the Spiritual Master (*Guru*) man learns to enter into good actions, and thereafter he starts understanding the grace of God. This world is a source of achieving right understanding. Understanding the reality of this world amounts to proceeding towards awakening and then its resultant is a life full of infinite peace, bliss and oneness with Everlasting Eternal Existence. Therefore, it is essential to take shelter in the Spiritual Master (*Guru*) and lead a life of renunciation in the quest of seeking the Truth. This is the greatest path for leading a purposeful life.

RECITATION OF GOD'S NAME

The great importance of God's name and the power of the Divine word is well established in different sections of religion (*Panth*). In the Indian philosophy the great faith in auspiciousness of name and its power to transform and direct towards Everlasting Eternal Existence, especially the tradition of greatness in God's name occupies such an important place that this methodology is complete in itself to touch greater heights in spirituality and experiencing God's existence. Besides *Gyanyog, Karmayog, Rajyog* and *Bhaktiyog*, the *Japyog*, practice of '*Divine Name*', is an important *Yog*. With *Japyog, Mantra-Jap* and *Naam-Jap* both are included. In *Kaliyug Naam-Jap* has special importance. God's name generates creative skills and bring speedy development in the *Sadhak*. In living a spiritual life equanimity is required in all parts of our existence. The entire

Although the saints who have attained the experience of inner wisdom and those who are *Shrotiya* and *Brahmanishtha* are enunciating and pronouncing about the *Ananda*, devotion and wisdom that takes one away from sensual pleasures and helps to live a life at higher level of consciousness; and it is visible all around that human being is engrossed in worldly pleasures to the same extent as he was centuries ago; and also human being is as inert and sleepy towards quest for life of consciousness as he was in the beginning of creation. Despite excited statements and believable assurances and self experiences of failures in the physical world in achieving happiness and pleasures man is repeatedly getting into deception, why it is so? Man has not yet learnt to tread on spiritual path, why it is so? Man listens to several spiritual discourses, reads spiritual literature and despite repeatedly listening to preachings, he does not do anything to practice; because he has no serious and stable faith in the preachings of noble men, in spiritual literature (*Dharma Scriptures*) and in the words of saints who have tread the path to attain *Anand*. He has faith in worldly pleasures and, therefore, he works for such outside pleasures. Man believes that money is required for happiness and joy. Man is filled with deep belief in temporary things. Thus, this is the reason of his misery. Due to lack of faith he remains deprived of the real joy of '*Sadhana*'. When man is ready to believe in impermanent humanly relationships, despite the fact the persons whom he believes die before him, it is not understood as to why he does not believe in God who has created that material object.

Keeping faith in the words of *Rishis*, Saints and preachings of the Spiritual Master (*Guru*) and understanding the importance of spiritual *Sadhana*, remembrance of God's name should be continuously practiced.

On the subject of Naam Goswami Tulsidas writes:

> *Naam prasad sambhu avinasi*
> *Saju amangal mangal rasi.*
> *Suk sankadik siddha muni jogi.*
> *Naam prasad Brahmasukha bhogi*

In this dreadful *'Kaliyug'* it is sufficient to know and believe that God in the form and name is a tree that grants all desires (*Krishna's Paradise*) and which can eradicate all sufferings and provide the desired results. In this *'Kaliyug'* action, devotion, wisdom are of lesser importance than remembrance of God's name and *Naam-Jap*.

There is a little difference between *Mantra-Jap* and prayer. To express your own emotions in any manner, in any language according to your preference is called prayer, whereas in *Mantra-Jap* words are to be recited following a particular manner. God's *Naam-japaam-Jap* is similar to fire; and which can bring control over all desires. *Mantra-Jap* gives wisdom and this wisdom is the result of the grace of God. Wisdom is nothing but realization of omnipresence of God. This is the highest intelligence. This helps eradication of worldly desires. The wish for experiencing God destroys all other desires. It is that wish which establishes everlasting kingdom of peace within. Just like a match-stick converts grass stack into ash, the one omnipresent, omnipotent and omniscient God is capable of destroying all worldly desires; because God is fulfillment of our wishes, and when we start feeling His presence there remains no desire to be fulfilled. *Mantra-Jap* or God's name remembrance is the base of realization of perennial (*Sanatan*) Existence of Everlasting Eternal power of God.

Naam-jap is also a *Yog*, because mind is to be fixed into *Mantra* recitation; diverting it from other sensualities. Naam-*Jap* and *Mantra-Jap* both are integrated in the process. There are many kinds of *Japa* for example, (i) daily *Japa*, (ii) periodical *Japa*, (iii) self interested *Japa*, (iv) prohibited *Japa*, (v) repentation *Japa*, (vi) changeless *Japa*, (vii) transient *Japa*, (viii) oral *Japa*, (ix) *Upanishu Japa* with movements of lips without sound being heard by any one. (x) *Japa* with bee-like sound, (xi) mental *Japa*, (xii) unbroken *Japa*, (xiii) *Japa* that is not recited, (xiv) *Japa* with circumambulation to the right, etc.

In oral *Japa* one can hear the sound outside. In *Upanishu Japa* there is the movement of lips but sound is not heard outside. In bee-like sound *Japa* there is no movement of lips. In mental *Japa*, there is meditation on the meaning of the words of *Mantra*. Unbroken *Japa* and *Japa* that is not recited are the *Japa* of simple *Sadhana* of saints. The *Sadhak* in beginning should start with oral *Japa* followed by *Upanishu Japa* After some time, the connection with external air diminishes in *Upanishu Japa*. But the real *Japa* is mental *Japa*, because the connection with external air gets delinked. In fact the distraction in mind comes through external air. Therefore in *Japa* the inhaling and exhaling process should be natural. Only in this state the connection with mind takes place. When in oral *Japa* the inhaling and exhaling process is normal, then oral *Japa* by itself gets converted into *Upanishu Japa*. In a similar manner *Upanishu Japa* gets converted into mental *Japa*, when the process of inhaling — exhaling slows down. In mental *Japa* one has to think of his idol and one can experience state of simple '*Samadhi*' (state of trance) which is a state of internal *Japa* going on automatically.

Oral and *Upanishu Japa* creates sound. In mental *Japa* the word and their meaning merge. After mental *Japa* when unbroken *Japa* starts then a state of meditation is achieved, where word and meaning become one. The state achieved in *Japa* is the normal state of saints. In this state *Japa* gets realized and one can see/experience the presence of Idol. All this happens in a state of particular sound. The Divine experience is also achieved in such a state because the state beyond is unexplainable.

In connection with *Japa* it is known that *Mantra* given by the Spiritual Master (*Guru*) or *Beeja Mantra* is specially useful, because these Mantras are awakened Mantras and through them 'Self' realization becomes easy. The names of God are also equally awakened like *Beeja Mantra*.

165

Therefore in *Kalikaal* recitation of names of God, Naam *Japa*, and remembrance of God's names are very important.

'Kalau Keshwakeertanaat' and *'Ramanaamnaiva Muktih syat Kalau Naaneyan Kenchit'* are the proof of the above expressions on *Japa*.

In Srimad Bhagvat it is written

'Kalau Yaddhari Keertanaat'.

Therefore *Sadhak* should establish himself in *Japa* of God's name.

Goswami Tulsidas in the importance of God's name has said:

'Nam let bhav sindhu sukhahein
Karahu vichara sujan maan manhein'.

of *Sanatan Dharma*, the universality of which needs no proof. (Upanishads, Srimad Bhagvat Gita, Srimad Bhagvatam, Brahm Sutra, Ramayan and many more Indian scriptures contain the very essence of Universal *Dharma*, Laws of Nature, Laws of Life, and Values of Life etc.)

One example is that of ancient Spiritual Master-Disciple (*Guru-Shishya*) relationship, which is most important and most valuable aspect of life for passing on of knowledge for prosperity, is getting seriously eroded in modern times indiscriminately.

The knowledge gained by communication system of *Guru-Shishya* tradition awakens the man to reach higher level of consciousness, because *Guru* himself has experienced the process. A common man can experience the eternal super consciousness through *Guru*'s Divine Grace. With the blessings, the grace, the benevolence, the compassion of *Guru* even the ignorant person can become master of his 'Self', leading towards expansive vision of consciousness/awareness. *Guru* is the medium to free you from fear, sorrow, pain, tension and stressful life and to let you enter into blissful and peaceful life. *Guru* is the basic forming link between man (Soul) and indestructible *'Tattva'* (Super Soul — God). A Divine *Guru* is an invaluable and unparalleled asset of Indian traditional cultural treasure, because only a Divine *Guru* has been entrusted with proprietary of the invaluable treasure of founder fathers of the spirituality that govern the Laws of Nature, Laws of Life and values of life and tells about the Ultimate Reality. He has most of the privileges as a custodian of the spiritual heritage of *Indian Sanatan Dharma* which is universally applicable. This outstanding *Guru — Shishya* tradition of India has passed on from generation to generation, the knowledge and direct experiences of the Rishis of the Upanishad times era with great care, effort, and discipline in an orderly and sequential manner. As a result of this organized tradition Bharat (India) has been crowned and adored as *Jagat Guru* (*Guru* of this world).

Despite many historical strong disturbances the National Unity has existed as a well knit garland of human values, humanity and love giving a vision of oneness. Today freedom of speech, criticism, argumentation and immodest behavior is seen all over. This is because man is ignorant about the meaning of human life and its purpose, as well as from the role and importance of *Guru* who awakens him to higher level of consciousness and brings enlightenment in respect of the Ultimate Reality. *Guru Tattva*, that is the energy of *Guru*, is blissful and provides permanent happiness. *Guru* is not merely a guide or teacher. His every word is Divine. He is Divine incarnation, his energy is endless/infinite (*'Anant/akhand'*). However, sadly enough, common man is not able to realize these aspects of Divinity in *Guru Tattva*.

It is for man now to realize the importance of the role of *Guru* in development of his level of material consciousness towards spiritual consciousness, that is indestructible Ultimate

Reality. Obviously *Guru Tattva* is the greatest of all that can take the man towards evolution of wisdom to realize the Truth. Adoration of *Guru* is actually worshipping God. From ancient times, Rishis, philosophers and thinkers have placed *Guru* on the highest platform equal to God. This is to clearing the mind from, doubt, unwillingness and fear and impart courage and maturity to human being for harnessing the fruits of worship and prayer and providing certainty of the results of persistent devotion and quest to know the everlasting non perishable cyclic existence.

"Guru Dev is Divine; Brahman,
We worship you Guru Dev".

All religious scriptures and great philosophers and thinkers tell us, that *Guru* is remover of ignorance (brings light in darkness) through his experiences and potential knowledge and wisdom. *Guru* is an oasis of kindness and destroyer of superficiality about spirituality. It is like an ambassador from Eternity. Just as an ambassador of a nation represents his nation in other country, *Guru* who has attained the state of perfect equanimity under all circumstances is a representative of the Divine. The honor of an ambassador of a nation is the honor of his nation. In a similar fashion honor to *Guru* (worship, prayer and service) is equal to worshipping the omnipresent, omnipotent, omniscient, everlasting existence, God, directly or indirectly. The presence of *Guru* in itself propounds fearlessly the existence of everlasting Eternal Truth. *Guru* is the permanent witness of God and in this ever-changing perishable worldly matter, he is local and vocal representative of God. A person can realize 'Self' through dedication and worship and following *Guru*'s instructions,

The world of experiences is very wide. A true seeker of the Truth is able to get many experiences of world beyond science. Many hints and messages can be received but only alert seekers get them. All this is possible only through kindness and grace of *Guru*. It must be taken as cent per cent true that glimpses of *Guru*, his grace, his gentle touch and kindness and one's determination brings many wonders; but it does not mean that seeker of the Truth becomes lazy and does not follow the prerequisites. A seeker should always have faith that his *Guru* is an infinite/boundless sea of kindness. In the words of Goswami Tulsidas it is '*Kripasindhu nar roop Hari*'. To get a *Shrotriya Brahmanishta* (learned and always in meditation of God) *Guru* is the greatest achievement of ones life. Leading successful spiritual life is only possible when a person is capable of rightly adjusting different facets of his personality and his complete personality with other matters of worldly affairs using wisdom and discrimination. In the light of this meaning life is an art of living. What does an artist do? An artist has a clear-cut imagination of his objective. He does accordingly to achieve it. He looks into the essential items and resources required; arranges them in an orderly manner. He then puts his natural imaginative vision into an art depicting his natural instinct. This is applicable to all great projects, whether they are art on canvas or art of making sculptures/idols or art of music or art of literature/poetry writing etc. The gist of art is to create naturality that depicts something beyond the matter and can easily make one feel/experience the existence beyond body. *Guru* is a spiritual artist. Just as an artist using material things create a live picture; *Guru* makes the inner-self of the disciple illuminative. *Guru* inspired with the inspiration of God, takes his disciple towards awakening. For a definite objective, God wants to get His work done through some medium. *Guru* is that medium. *Guru* provides direction to his disciples for the objectives and plans as per the wishes of God.

'Ishwara gururatmeyti murtibhed vibhagne'.

God, *Guru* and Soul are the three different forms of the same eternal power (the Eternal Truth). This Eternal power at a fixed point of time exposes herself through the above three forms and comes into Being.

The eternal power (the Ultimate Reality) that appears in the form of God, *Guru* and Soul is one and the same in all the forms and gets the work done through them. This Ultimate Reality is infinitely pleasant, peaceful and pure. The above three forms are working force of the Eternal power. In the form of *Guru*, She removes the darkness of ignorance from the mind of the disciple and kindles light of wisdom in him. *Guru* is present in manifested form. *Guru* is the center of full spiritual powers. When the disciple comes in contact with *Guru* often, he starts getting spiritual experiences. The disciple (the *Sadhak*) when comes in close contact with *Guru* regularly, he starts getting Divine powers within by the grace of *Guru* and the powers of *Guru* start flowing into the *Sadhak*. This is a form of transmutation of power or phase entanglement of energy. Those disciples who keep and remember *Guru* in their heart persistently, also have every chance of transmutation of energy. Rendering service and following instructions (with full faith) of a S*hrotriya* and *Brahmnisth Guru* act like a medicine for curing the worldly attractions. As a seeker (of the Truth) our intelligence lies in following the instructions of *Guru* with full belief and faith for self-awakening and enlightenment. It is the experience of a true seeker that one should follow the instructions and preachings of *Guru*, so as to care and share with those who are less lucky.

Once a *Sadhak* told that in this modern era it is not possible to get a Shrotriya Brahmnistha *Guru*. No doubt, it is difficult to get such a *Guru*, but to get a true seeker is still more difficult. Can a patient just entering into the clinic of a doctor guess the ability of the doctor? Ignorant disciples who know little about the spiritual road, start judging the saints in the very beginning. And most of them, based on their poor judgment, dissociate themselves from the learned *Guru* because they make the judgment on the basis of outer environment around.

Guru's knowledge is entirely different than his outer environment. What is in there in *Guru*'s heart and what wisdom lies in him? If the *Sadhak* cannot judge, he remains far away from *Guru* though he may be very near to him. Wisdom and spiritual experiences are absolutely internal state. Very often *Guru* does behave like a common man. It is difficult to assess the depth of his internal state of wisdom based on his outer state. Be alert! A disciple should be polite, truthful and faithfully serve the *Guru*.

Guru is not merely a physical being. *Guru* is energy and he is considered *Param Brahman*, the Divine consciousness.

Rishis have defined sacredness of *Guru*:

> '*Dhyan Moolam Guru Murti, Puja Moolam Guru Padam, Mantra Moolam Guru Vakayam, Moksha Moolam Guru Kripa*'. This means that root of meditation comes from *Guru*, worship comes from *Guru*'s lotus feet, root of *Mantra* is *Guru*'s word, and root of nirvana is *Guru*'s blessings.

DIVINE WISDOM

C hurning of mind is essential duty of all human minds. It is the origin of Divine treasure. The mind is struggle place of demons and gods (wrong and right). Vedas have described the human body akin to pitcher and ocean : *'Purusho vai samudrah'*.

If the demons get installed in life force, man starts his journey towards perishment. In this body the main place of energy is in nerve network. It has two parts (i) mind (ii) spinal cord nerve, which is known as *'Sushumna'* in yogic language. According to a learned person, head is the origin of entire life force (*'Pran'*)

'Shira vai Prananam yoni'

The five life forces are the driver of five sensual organs. They are controlled by head.

In etymological interpretation of words especially as to do with Vedic compositions, it is said:

'Yachchhiyam samdohastsmchchirah
tasminnetasmin prana
ashryant tasmada ou yeva yetat shirah'

God exploited the three objects of life (*Kaam, Arth, Dharma*). '*Pran*' (life breath) took shelter in head. Being a shelter head got this name. The three objects of life, shelter and head all contain the different forms of original element '*Shrimshrayane*'. Vedas mention this. head or mind is the birth place of life force (*Pran*). Another name of mind — '*Chamas*' (a vessel) is detailed in Vedas.

Upnishads and '*Vedamantra*' also describe about '*Chamas*', whose mouth is downwards and bottom upwards. An inspection of our body reveal the same thing — the head is situated at the upper part of spinal cord. The upper part of spinal cord is called '*Sumeru*' (the sacred mountain *Meru* of north pole) and the lower part is called as '*Kumeru*' (south pole). In between these two the continuous life force is running; this is the base of our health and longevity of life. Head is also called '*Kalash*' (pitcher) which is full of nectar (*Somras*). In our body the inhaling action is going on uninterruptedly. The mind fully filled with '*Somras*' (the nectar juice that was given to Gods during vedic sacrifices) is the place of wisdom/knowledge / intelligence in which the entire nerves system remains irrigated. It gets generated in the tank of mind. It nourishes and purifies the subtle nerves of mind and *'Sushumna'* and is found everywhere in the body. In Rigveda *'Som'* is called the juice of *'Indra'* related to sensual organs. The lord of sensual organs — mind — is *'Indra'* — *'Som Indiro Ras'* and point where these two meet is called 'Aakash' (Space). Our entire sensual activities are dependent upon the cooperation of the above three (i.e. *Sushumna*, mind and space). The outcome of treasure by churning the ocean is connected with internal elements of man's body; in terms of spirituality. *'Som'* or moon is *'Somras'* which flows the elixir element. Longevity of life, *'Pran'* (life force), awareness, light, Divine power are the elixir. In Vedas these are called *'Amritroop'* (the forms of elixir).

Semen is based on water element. It has been made clear in 'Aitreya Upnishad' — *'Aapah reto bhutva shishnam praptishaat'*. The semen is synonymous to power. In semen, life force and air are of the highest order. It has two forms. One is godly and the other demonly. Born out of water the *'Sattavik'* form is elixir and *'Tamsik'* form is poison. In Vedas elixir is called *'Som'* and poison is called wine (alcohol). *'Sattavik'* element is elixir and *Tamsik* element is wine.

> *'Prajapaterva aitey andhsi yatsomashch*
> *Sura cha*
> *Tat satayam sri jyotih somah amritah*
> *papma tamah Sura'*

Lord has two types of food —'*Som* and *Sura*'. Truth, light, are called '*Som*'. Lie, sin and darkness are called '*Sura*'. Both are present in human body. The power in the body that we get from food is '*Sura*' and that creates dullness. The subtleness of other secretions creates subtle mind and they are called '*Som*'. '*Som*' is moon which is said to be born from mind:

'*Chandrama manso jatah*'

In spirituality area, moon means mind; which decreases and increases in form, determination and alteration. '*Som*' is the moon that provides nectar of peace in mind. In churning of the ocean '*Som*' (nectar) came out and was made available to Gods through the Sun God. In Atharva Veda mind is termed as heaven.

'*Ashtachakra navdwara devanom purayodha
Asyam hiranaya to koshah swargo jyotshavratah*'.

This human body, having eight chakras and nine sensual organs, is a treasure of gold (*Hiranya*) which is hidden by light. This mind is lighted heaven (*Devalok*). '*Hiranya*' also means life force, semen and nectar and the mind is the treasure. Mind is a place of definite intentions (resolutions). The desire of '*Kaam*' generates from mind; and therefore it is called — originated from mind. When it reaches at the stage of intellect, then it brings out resolutions; and due to which there is loss of semen from mind.

Mind can only be controlled through worship — yoga. Mind becomes changeless (as the ultimate being) and *Kaam* is under control. According to Indian scriptures (*'Shashtra'*) Divine wisdom is referred to as Light, the rays of which spread all over, destroying darkness and ignorance. In our body only mind is capable of thinking, the body below the head is incapable of thinking — Rishis have called head as *'Devalok'* or *'Jyotirlok'* and remaining body is called *'Tamolok* or *Asurlok'*. In human being both Gods and demons reside together. One who applies wisdom and understands the difference he leads a happy life. *'Sushumna'* is known as earth and head/mind is heaven. The opposite pairs elixir — poision and *'Som — Sura'* are the indicators of behavioral state of mind. The controller of life force (*'Pran'*) is mind. This seven faced mind is the vehicle horse of Gods. Acheiving control over seven faced sensual conduct of mind or turning it inwards, the Gods occupy desired place. In *'Kathopnishad'* sensual organs have been similarised with horse.

A great importance has been given to *'Horse Indra'* produced at the churning of mind; meaning thereby that *Mantra*, *Katha* and listening are similar to the conduct of *'Horse* of *Indra'*. Our firm determination power is divine *'Kaustubh Mani'* (the jewel worn by Lord Krishna on his breast) which is an ornament of heart. A person without firm determination power is without prosperity, success, happiness. Lord Vishnu also possesses the '*Kaustubh Mani*' in his heart. The collective power of mind-intellect — *Chitta* — ego (all the four) has been designated as vehicle of '*Indra*'. The Soul has her full '*Indra*' and in contact with that our sensual organs function. '*Indra*' is the middle '*Pran*' (life force) which is responsible for prosperity of sensual organs.

> *Sa yoapam madhya pranah. yesh avam*
> *'Indraha'.*
> *Tanesh pranam madhyat indraiyan*
> *tadendha samadighdha.*
> *Egdhe havain ityachakshte pariksham.*

'*Indra power*', appears in the form of determination power. Man himself is Lord Vishnu and *Yagya*. The five sensual organs are called five classes of Being (gods, men, gandharvas, apsaras, snakes and spirits of ancestors). Their conversation medium is sound of '*Shankh*' (a kind of a shell that can create sound on blowing air into it by mouth).

The lack of restraint of sensual organs is undebatable (beyond doubt). The bondage of sensual organs with mind in the thread of wisdom is Divine and sweet sound of 'Panchjanya *Shankh*'. Controlled sensual organs are like '*Kamdhenu*' — a cow of plenty (a fabulous cow produced at churning of ocean and supposed to yield whatever is required — mythology). The man with Divine conduct gets blessed in serving '*Kamdhenu*', this is sacrificial enjoyment. The enjoyment power of sensual organs and indisciplined man, inhales/ drinks blood, which is demon like, conduct.

With determination, good intention, faith and belief and hardwork nothing is impossible in this world. Thought and discriminating power comes from mind. Mind has been designated heaven. *'Kalpvriksha'* (a tree that grants all desires/ Krishna's paradise) is a heavenly tree; it is also called *'Parijaat'*. It sprouts in man as soon as he takes birth. This thought — tree does sequential inauguration of inner strengths of mind. The child and adult are the stages of the same. Thoughts, respectively, are based on intelligence. People having righteously developed mind possess firm determination power. They under the shadow of *'Kalpvriksha'* fulfill their desires, because their conduct of mind remains balanced (state of equanimity).

EXPERIENCING GOD

Among the methods described in Indian Scriptures prayer/worship is the best approach to attain Divine closeness to God. In order to attain goodness, purity and higher consciousness, *Shruti* enunciates:

> *Atmetyevopasi tadamanamevavet,*
> *Tamer viditvaatimratyumeti naanyh*
> *pantha vidyateynam*

Worship God to please God. Having understood the name and form of God, *'Jiva'*, in this death certain world, can win over worldly pleasures. There is no other way.

Why there is so much unhappiness and uncalmness in this entire Nature? Numerous planets, sub-planets, moon, sun and stars, from times immemorial, are in motion in infinite space in accordance with Nature but in which eternal everlasting existence it is desirous to get dissolved? Why there is so much chaos in the entire world? Which everlasting eternal omnipresent existence putting chain of attraction — repulsion among these planets and sub-planets is keeping them in motion? Under the influence of same attraction-repulsion which omniscient *'Purush'*, from times immemorial, is holding this phenomenal world keeping *'Jive-Jagat'* in motion with attachment and envy?

While delayering this mystery of God play the disciplined noble men must have come to know, that as if numerous pure rivers of worship are flowing with great force towards the ocean of *Sat-chit-Anand* (existence-knowledge-bliss).

> *Yatha nadyah spandmanah samudrastam*
> *gachchhanti namrupe vihaye,*
> *Tatha vidwannamrupadwamuktah*
> *paratmram*
> *purushmupaiti divyam.*

(Just like flowing rivers when get into the sea renounce their identity and existence, the learned and *Brahmanishth* person, in a similar manner, become one with Brahman leaving ignorance of *'Maya'* of name and form). *Maya* means illusion.

This kind of pilgrimage of ocean like Brahman is not only present in world of awareness (*Chetan* world) but it is also present in the gross world of Nature of material awareness. This is because the aim of every chaotic state is to attain calmness. When the aim of every unpeaceful state is to transform into a peaceful state, then

183

the unpeaceful state of the entire world will be eager to merge with Brahman; where is the doubt in it? The entire materialistic world being the result of natural changes and resonance of three *Gunas (Sattva, Rajas, Tamas)* is ever playful. That is why nothing in this world of Nature is still and conjugated with everlasting peace.

This peace is beyond materialistic Nature. This peace exists only in Brahman which signifies oneness and it is beyond the kingdom of changing Nature. Therefore, whatever efforts we do to experience oneness, i.e., Brahman are called worship. In Veda, *Karmakanda, Upasanakanda,* and *Gyankanda* have been mentioned for worshipping God (*Sat-chit-Anand*) with name and form. God Shri Hari is full of *Sadbhava, Chidbhava,* and *Anandbhava.* The Upasanakanda of Veda is connected with *Anandbhava* of God. Shri Hari (*Parmatma*) is in the form of *Anand.* The meaning God is — infinite *Anand.*

> *Raso vay sah Anandam brahmoti*
> *vyajanat,*
> *Anand rupam param yuddhibhati Anand*
> *Bramano vidwan na vibheti kutashch na*
> *Anandadadheya khalvimani bhutani*
> *jayanne*
> *Ananden jatani jevanti Anandam*
> *prayantaybhivishanteeti*

God is the dense form of *Anand,* sweet *Anand* which is inexhaustible and everlasting. Shri Hari is the original source of such *Anand.* Brahman is

Anand. When *'Jiva'* attains Brahman *Anand,* then his localized fear is destroyed. The creation of world lies in God Shri Hari and so is destruction/ dissolution. The entire creation belongs to God/ *Anand.*

All the living beings are created by *Anand* (God). Shri Hari protects the entire world with this *'Anand Roop* and in *'Anandamayi Jagdishwar'* all the living beings get dissolved and merged.

The *Anandamayi* existence of Shri Hari in the entire world provides joy and pleasure which is nothing but presence of infinite *Anand.* One's belief/faith or otherwise is the cause of differences. Shri God Hari is an ocean of *Anand.* From the same ocean of *Anand,* drawing drop by drop various kinds of *Anand* have been created in this *'Jiva-Jagat'* (world) : For parents *Anand* of love for the child, in the heart of child *Anand* of respect for parents, in the mind of husband *Anand* of love for his wife, in the mind of wife *Anand* of sweetness for husband, in the still mind and heart of *Sadguru Anand* of compassion for the disciple, etc., all are drenched in the stream of *Anand* of Shri Hari. As the pure ever flowing Bhagirathi Maa coming out in the form of a stream from the lotus feet of Shri Hari dividing herself into hundreds of streams is making the entire Universe pure and pious, in a similar way she is making pure and pious the various forms of God Shri Hari, namely, *Anandrupi, Mandakini* and other materialistic pleasure forms of *Maya* — the phenomenal world — somewhere appearing in the form of faith, somewhere in the form of love and somewhere in the form of devotion.

This *Anand* is distracted in two ways. One is through *Chitta* in the form of blissful knowledge and other through *Maya*, ignorance in the form of sensual pleasures. In this visibly perceived outer world the various sensual pleasures, they being connected with *Maya*, are also the images of *Brahmananda*. The difference in light of Sun and that of the image of Sun in water compares to the same extent with the sensual pleasures derived in images of *Brahmananda*. When the *Anand* existence of Shri Hari is under the influence of *Maya*'s *Tamasik* matter, then there is no pure *Anand* and it is called dirty sensual pleasure. When the same *Anand* existence leaving dirty *Tamsik* and *Rajsik* kingdom gets kindled by *Sattavik* kingdom, there its true form (*Brahmananda*) makes the heart of devotee full with happiness and *Anand*. Among all the pleasures/joys, the real pleasure and joy (*Anand*) is the *Anand* kingdom of Shri Hari.

The various attributes of *Maya*, in different conditions, influence the man differently; and when the kingdom of *Maya* disappears, then the pure *Brahmananda* kindles. Righteous people experience the light within, that kindles as *Brahmananda*.

The sensual pleasures are just shadow of the *Brahmananda*. Taking shadow as the Truth, reflection as reality and the visible world as the Truth, '*Jiva*' lives in ignorance. In the kingdom of Nature whatever sensual pleasures we see are just the feeling of *Brahmananda*; because when this world is the creation of *Anand* then any kind of pleasure cannot be different than *Anand*.

'*Bhagavati Shruti*' says:

> *Eshoasya parmanand*
> *etasyevaanandsyanyani bhutani*
> *bhagmupjeevanti*

This is *Anand* of Brahman. All other living beings live in this world having a part of the same Brahman in them.

PARA *SHAKTI* DIVINE NATURE MOTHER

Since beginning of the creation, the tradition of worshipping all powerful Divine Nature Mother is being practiced. The whole symbolic world represented — Trinity of the Divine Nature Mother (*Mattra Shakti*), the Absolute (Shiv) and Love (Krishna, Radha). *Mattra Shakti* is being worshipped as sovereign deity. There is no such part of life that has not been illuminated by *Mattra Shakti* right from the beginning of life and developments thereafter. She has always been an essential part in the form of mother; in giving birth and nurturing, human being. In Indian philosophy Divine Mother Nature is '*Shakti*' and that is why '*Shakti*' stands at first place in this world. The humble tradition of worshipping mother started under Indian philosophy.

In course of time worshipping mother converted into worshipping *'Shakti'*. It was not only prevalent in India, but it was practiced in other countries as well, e.g China, Egypt, South America, Tibet etc. In India worshipping *'Mattra Shakti'* is placed at the top platform.

> *Sarvdevmayi devi sarvdevimayam jagat*
> *Atoaham vishwaroop namami*
> *permeshwarim*

From the centers of ancient Bharat (India), among the statues found in Mohenjo-Daro Haddappa the majority of the statues were of women having deer like eyes. In Vedic era the importance of male deities appeared more than that of female deities. In Vedic Dharma the early morning hours were considered like female deities. In *'Vaaka Sukta'*, *'Devi Sukta'* and *'Raat Sukta'* of Rigveda, word, earth and night have been symbolized as female deities and to worship them *'Mantra'* were composed. In Rigved Sun has been addressed as mother of continuum world. Having known earth as mother, the son of earth considered himself blessed. In Atharvaveda the earth is the mother of human being, and therefore in all walks of life the earth has been accepted as *'Devi'* (Female deity/*Shakti*) of protection. Atharvaveda has mentioned about a *Devi* deity (*Shakti*) called *Viraj*. She is the mother of the three *Lokas*. She has been connected with Sun. She has also been called as *'Swaha'*. The Vedic tradition has made exceedingly important contribution in worshipping mother '*Shakti*' (woman power). In post-vedic era scriptures, the names Ambika, Uma, Durga, Kali, etc, have been mentioned as mother '*Shakti*' and have been worshipped with great devotion and reverence. In '*Vaajsaneyee Sanhita*' and in '*Taittriya Brahaman*' *Ambika* has been called as wife of Rudra (Shiv). In Kain Upnishad, Uma has been called a form of entire '*Brahmna – Vidya*' (Absolute knowledge). In *Mundako Upnishad*, it is stated that Fire has seven tongues — *Kali, Karali, Manojava, Sulohita, Sudhumra Varna,. Sphuluigani and Vishwaruchi.* '*Suttra*' literature indicates Durga as the first name, who has been described as wife of Rudra (Shiv). In '*Guhaya Suttra*' *Durga, Bhadrakali* and *Bhavani* have been described as the creator and ruler of the world.

The '*Mahati Swaroop*' (All powerful) of *Shakti* has been picturised in '*Durga Strotam*' and '*Harivansh Puran's* ' *Aryastavana* (Prayer/Verses) of Mahabharat. A study of this reveals that Durga *Devi* in this immeasurable form is a *Vedic Tattva* on one side and on the other she is also beyond *Vedic Tattva*. The names: Arya, Kaushitki, Katayayni point towards Vedic tradition. On the other side the Berber, Shavar, Pulinds (Tribes) worshipped Mother *Shakti*. They were also called Arpana, Nagnashari, Parnabhri. This has an indication towards post-vedic tradition. The importance of *Devi* worship in '*Pauranic*' era is amply exemplified in the '*Devi Mahatam Khand*' of '*Markandeya Puran*'. The principle of Nature (Prakriti) and '*Purush*' of sankhaya philosophy is symbol of the same Eternal *Shakti Jagadambha*.

In 'Durga Strota' of 'Bhishmaparva' and 'Viratparva' of epic Mahabharat, the separate entity of Devi Shakti has been registered. In 'Harivarsh Puran' 'Kaushiki Devi' has been mentioned as daughter of Yashoda. 'Bhavani', 'Sharvani', 'Rudrani' and 'Mranani' names of Devi have been mentioned in 'Panini'. Kautilya (Chanakya) in his economics has discussed about the temple Devi Madira alongwith invincible Gods in the chapter 'Durg – Nivesh'. In fact Durga is the foundation of creation Shakti (Omnipotent) of the world. Durga is present as 'Sattaviki Shakti' in Vishnu, 'Rajasi Shakti' in Brahma and 'Tamsi Shakti' in Shiv. The creation Shakti of Brahma, the preserving Shakti of Vishnu, the light Shakti of Sun, the burning Shakti of Fire and the Inspirational Shakti of Air is all nothing but Durga everlasting Eternal Shakti. There are several names of this Shakti, e.g, Ambika, Durga, Katayayni, Mahisasurmardani, Narayani, Gauri, etc. Skandpuran says that Shiv without Shakti is like a corpse. Shiv Tattva as Shiv comes out only in conjuction and association with MahaShakti.

> Jagatkarnmapannh shivo yom
> munirattamh
> Tasyapi namvachchhkriyastya heeno
> nirarthakah

Vedas while worshiping Devi (Shakti) have averred, Hay! Devi you are 'Mahamaya'. Creation of world is your Nature. The entire world is seen because of you. In Omkar you are half Maya and in Gayatri you are Om. There is a mention in

Bangla scripture that before the creation of the world once *Brahma, Vishnu and Mahesh* (*Shiv*) were worshipping the '*Sanatan*' (perennial) *Shakti* on the bank of river 'Ganga', *Devi* came near them in the form of a rotten corpse. First Vishnu got so much disturbed with the foul smell, that He stood up immediately. Then Brahma turned His face on the right side to avoid foul smell. As a result Brahma got two faces and He was getting foul smell from both sides. Like this as Brahma turned His face on four sides He got four faces and foul smell troubled Him so much that He ran away from worshipping. *Shiv* remained and continued worshipping. *Shakti* was pleased with *Shiv* and He became '*Panchmukhi*'. Since ancient times for worshipping *Shakti* fifty one temples were established from Baluchistan to Assam and Kashmir to Kanyakumari. Rules were formed for visiting worshipping those sacred places. This implies that *Shakti* is all, in all, without *Shakti* neither we can think nor can we understand. Without *Shakti* neither can we stand up nor can we walk. Senses and *Pran* are also the result of *Shakti*. Electrical *Shakti* (energy), attraction *Shakti*, meditation *Shakti*, etc, are the expressions of *Shakti*.

Through *Sattva, Raja and Tama*, *Shakti* does Her work. For the creation of this material world the five elements space (Akash), air, fire, water and earth are Her resource. Earth, water, fire, air, aakash, mind, intellect and ego all put together are called gross or '*Apara Prakriti*' (Nature). *Apara Prakriti* is of a lower order and acts as bondage for the world. '*Para Prakriti*' is pure. She Herself is Soul-'Self'. She forms and hold the life. She has entered the whole world and holds the existence of the world. This is also called '*Chaitanya' Prakriti* or Live force.

Maya, Mahamaya, Original *Prakriti, Avidya, Vidya*, Visible, Invisible, *Kundalini, Maheshwari*, Everlasting Eternal *Shakti*, Permeshwari, Jagdishwari, *Tamas*, Ignorance, are all synonyms to *Shakti. Navdurga, Kali, Asthalaxmi, Nashakti, Devi*, etc, are the exposition of *Para Shakti. Mahalaxmi, Mahasaraswati* and *Mahakali* are the three main visible forms of *Shakti*. A study of *Devi sutak* in the tenth section of Rigveda clearly reveals that in the basic element of God, man and animal, *Mahashakti* is the principal expression. This *Mahashakti* is Durga having lion as vehicle, which with cooperation of different *Shakits* joint together in numerous hands destroys demons, like laziness and ignorance. The *Devi* make us feel Her *Kaal* form.

This Godly *Shakti* in the form of *Kaal* is continuously changing the existence of matter, we all experience in this continually changing world as matter. There are two Navratras — *Chaitra Navaratra* and *Ashwin Navaratra* is principal '*Kaal Samvantar'*. These are respectfully called *Rama Navaratra* and *Durga Navaratra* or Spring Navaratra and winter Navaratra. On these occasions we see *Mahashakti* in the form of visible changes in the climate, flora and fauna etc. *Durga Navaratra* is the most important *Kaal* of Prayer and worship of *Shakti*. Here it is sufficient to say that this phenomenal world appears from Mother Durga, grows and then dissolves into Durga. Thus *Durga* is mother, Protector *Devi* also and is basal point of *Shakti*. We all bow our head, pray and worhip *Durga Shakti*.

> *Ya Devi sarvabhuteshu shaktiruepen*
> *sansthita*
> *Namastasyai namastasyai namastasyai*
> *namo Namah*

INCARNATION

Omnipotent, omnipresent formless God taking incarnation in the form of worldly body of flesh is a Divine order. Several kinds of inquisitiveness come into the minds of the Sadhaks regarding God incarnates. God being devoid of any wish in this being, how the desire comes in Him to manifest Himself as a worldly person and perform actions like common man/ woman? Being free from Maya how can formless God manifest Himself in the form of body of flesh? The omnipresent God, who is not bound by 'Deshkaal material', how and from where He comes? Because if He is present at one place and not present at another place it is understood that He comes from the place where He was present, but He being omnipresent, how it is possible to say that He is coming from a particular place? Supposedly even if we believe God's incarnation, it does not clarify as to what is the purpose of His manifestation as body of flesh? When God is omnipotent, then He can simply with wish destroy the devils/demons and protect His worldly creation. Like this, several enquiries appear in the minds of the *Sadhak*s in quest of seeking the Truth (God) on the subject of God's incarnation. Rigveda says about God's incarnation:

> *Rupam rupam tartirupo vabhut rupam*
> *prachchanay,*
> *Indra mayabhih pururup eyate yukta*
> *hayaya haryah shota dash*

God on listening to the prayers of devotees takes the human body or any other living body for the sake of those devotees who have pure souls and who love him, God has hundreds of forms, out of which His ten forms as God incarnate are the main ones.

Yajurveda describes God's incarnation as:

> *Prajapatikshehrati garbheanter jayanmani*
> *bahudha vijay*

Lord Prajapati takes birth in womb. Though there is no actual birth of Lord Prajapati, He appears in many different forms. Only patient yogis can understand the Divine grace of His appearance in various forms. The entire world is within Him.

In the '*Tenth Skandh*' of '*Srimad Bhagvat*' Maharshi Ved Vyas writes about the incarnation of '*Sri Hari*' —

Vibharshi rupanyavbodh Atma kshemaye
lokasya characharsya
Satvopapannani sukhavahani
satambhadhranio much lakhanam.

For the protection of the phenomenal world God with all attributes takes form. The God incarnates provide happiness to religious persons and destroy devils and demons.

Though unborn, yet God with the help of *Maya* takes form in the world as God incarnate who is also the controller of all elements. As and when there is decline in *Dharma* and there is prosperity of Ad*harma*, Shri Hari takes incarnation in the form of body to protect saints, destroy sinners and to reestablish *Dharma* order according to the then prevailing situations. God, being self illuminating, is omnipresent. Incarnation means taking form, which represent God as omnipotent, omnipresent and omniscient. Omnipresent God can appear in any form, anytime, at any place to save His devotees and enlighten them. Being omnipresent He is omnipotent. God is the base of all the strengths and power. In the glory of God in Srimad Bhagvat it is said:

'From the inspiration of the omnipotent God all the living beings of entire world derive their life force and acquire wisdom and happiness. Further, on whom the entire world continuously cycles like a mustard seed, we offer our prayer, worship

**and devotion to Him (the infinite, all
powerful God).'**

Shwetashavtara Upanishad describes as to
how God's power expands all over in the Global
world.

> *Ya eko varno bahudha*
> *shaktiyogyadadhrannaekan*
> *nihitartho dadhati*
> *Yo devoagnau yoapsu yo vishvam*
> *bhuvanmavivinsh*
> *Ya aushdhishu yo vanaspatishu tasmai*
> *devay namonamah*

Oneness and God's lone omnipotence has lead
to creation and expansion of diverse and different
creatures. The above said power of God has Her
expression in fire, water, medicinal herbs and
vegetative kingdom; meaning thereby it is present
all over in the entire world. Brahman is complete
with power that is omnipotent. When this power
is expressed through an outside scene, then the
outside world gets lighted to be visibly seen. This
expansive power of God in Indian scriptures
is called *Kalaa* (Art/play). It is said where
complete sixteen Art/Play become luminous and
expansive, there sixteen *Kalaa Shakits* appeared in
phenomenal world. Just as full Moon is said to be
complete with sixteen Arts, the full power of God
is called *Shakti* of sixteen Arts. This is why God is
complete with sixteen Arts.

There are sixteen Arts of God. The sixteen Arts of God (*kalaa Shakti*) exist in the entire world both living and non-living. As the life steps up the ladder of evolution the Art of God with the help of *Jiva* also develops and evolves. This can be taken as that the extent of evolution in the Art of God is direct index for the state of development / evolution of *Jiva*. With this process of evolution/ development of Art of God, *Jiva* of one form transforms into another form depending upon the development of Art accomplished by the *Jiva*. In the context of *Jiva Tattva*, this science has already been proved that in the creation of phenomenal world the creator comes first and the creation afterwards. Out of sixteen Arts of God, development of first one Art will be through a creature having *Annamaya kosh* (stomach) – that is aquatic creation. This principle has been established. *Shruti* has also evidenced and proved this principle. In Chhadyogyopnishad it is written:

> *Shodshanam kalanameka kalalishishtabhut*
> *Soanenopas mahita prajwalit*

Out of sixteen Arts of God, the first one Art, after getting mixed with food, was revealed through *Annamaya kosh*. Therefore, among the various forms of existence only those forms that have *Annamaya kosh* (Stomach) reveal first one Art of God. This form of existence that have *Annamaya kosh* is an aquatic creature. This principle is established. In this way the creatures coming in wet condition that is insects, etc., have two Arts of God; the creatures taking birth through egg have three Arts of God and animals have four Arts of God. Thereafter *Jiva* coming into the form of human being. In the human being the development of Art of God varies between five to eight. Ordinary persons have five Arts of God and spiritually developed have eight.

In the way beginning with one Art of God up to eight Arts of God, the development of eternal power is in a worldly manner; meaning thereby upto half of full Eternal power, the development is of worldly order. Thereafter, beginning from nine Arts of God to sixteen Arts of God, the centers of development of Eternal power come under the category of *Avtar* (God Incarnation). It is possible that the *Avtars* may not look like human beings and may be in the forms of life below the level of human being; but being the centers of Eternal power they are extraordinary centers.

mind of Narad. But the same grandeur in the mind of Kuber's sons Nalkuber and Manigreev was creating sensual pleasures. Their self willed unrestrained intention of sensual pleasure was becoming the cause of development of demon-like character and conduct; the same situation at the same time was transforming into elixir and poison as well. The charming and beautiful nature was creating devotion for God and the same nature was activating enjoyment for sensual pleasures in the worldly mind of sons of kuber. Narada, with divine hope of God's grace was proceeding towards *Narayan Ashram* (God's place of residence). Suddenly compassionate emotions started coming into his mind. In heart filled with endless compassion Narad experienced generous emotions. Nalkuber and Manigreeva, gathering a group of fairies, and having intoxicating alcoholic drink were wandering unrestrained insanely; spoiling the ever pure Tapovan of Chandramanlishwara. In a moment the fairies derobed themselves and Nalkuber and Manigreeva also decloathed themselves. They all entered in the pure stream of Mother Mandakini river and started playing in the water without any restraint and forgetting themselves, they were behaving improperly. By chance through the same shore Devrishi Narada was starting towards Narayan *Ashram* and the fairies in bare bodies had a glance towards Narada. All were ashamed and in doubt of getting cursed ran out of the pure stream of Mandakini river and in embarrassment immediately put on their Cloathes. Nalkuber and

Manigreeva blinded by desire started shouting eagerly in uncloathed state raising both the hands to call the fairies to enter again in the pure stream. They did not notice the divine presence of Narada. A man full of sensual desires is not able to see even nearby things. A man keen of sensual desires is like a blind man. He cannot see anything except sensual desires.

An infinite Divine power turned Narada's sight towards them. Narada saw their condition. Narada's heart got filled with compassion. Oh! Such a decline and degeneration of Kuber's sons.

Immediately Devrishi Narada made arrangements for their purification and for the end of their continuous worldly stream of life and death cycle. Narada by hiding his Divine grace in the garb of anger cursed them.

'Atoahantah sthavartam syatam naiv
yatha punah.
Smritih syanmatprasaden tattrapi
madgrahat punah.
Vasudevasya sanidhyam labdhwa
divyasharchchhate.
Vratte swalokantam bhuyo labdhbhakti
bhavishyatah.'

In conformity to your inertness and stupidity you become *Yamlarjuna* tree and stand for hundred God years. Even after becoming tree your memory will not vanish, sons of Kuber. With my grace you will throughout remember your past life. Then

after hundred God years with the touch of the feet
of Krishna you will get blessed.

Kuber's sons started waiting:

> God's incarnation, incarnation
> means appearance in form, coming
> down on earth of *Param Brahman*.
> God is omnipresent, omnipotent, and
> omniscient and is always present
> everywhere but has hid himself with
> his self charming magical power
> (*Maya*).

On his own desire, sometimes, removing this
cover of his own *Maya* he comes in this earthy
world.

This is His incarnation—Leelavtar, Kartavatar,
Gunavatar, Yugavatar, Anshavatar, Arthavatar
etc. All these *Avtars* (incarnation) are complete in
all respect.

> '*Purnanandah purna bhukta.*
> *Purnakarta purugyanah purnabha*
> *purnashaktih.*
> *Purnashwarayad Bhagwan Vasudev*
> *Virudha*
> *Shaktinam ch dhoshprageeshah.*'

God possesses everlasting complete *Anand*,
enjoyment, dutifulness, wisdom, light, power,
divine majesty, opposite—power—element,
guiltless touch.

Kuber's sons started waiting for the incarnation of God who is complete in all respects mentioned above. And then the Divine incarnation of compassionate God-In the title of the present period, in the last phase of *Dwapar yug* (one among the four *Yug – Satyug, Tretayug, Dwaparyug, Kaliyug*) at midnight of dark night of Bhadramas – at a place that is, cruel Kansa's prison, Rohini Nakshatra, Ashtamitithi, the loving night of dark night king, justice loving Budha planet, spiritual and Dhramapradhan lagan – Vrash – in such a blissful time the greatest light appeared removing the dense darkness of night.

> *'Nishithe tam udbhute jayamane*
> *janardhana*
> *Devkyam devrupinyam Vishnuh sava*
> *guhashyah,*
> *Aviraseed yatha prachyam dishinoduriv*
> *pushkal.*

The appearance of great light from the darkness and Devaki and Vasudeva are unaware of the sudden appearance of God Vishnu. God in order to fulfill his vow (assertion) came into the womb of Devaki. *Shiv*, Brahma, Narad, and other gods alongwith Rishis, Munis came to the prison in Mathura.

> *'Satyvratam satyaparam satayasya*
> *yonim trihitam ch sateye*
> *Satyasya satayammratsatya netram*

*satya sateye tamakam tvam sharnam
prapanna'.*

O! Lord you are devoted to a vow of
truthfulness
your vow, assertion is Truth
your vow, assertion is everlasting
Truth
you are on Truth.
The source and methodology to
attain you is Truth
you are trinity of Truth, the past, the
present
and the future.
You are truth in all three periods
You are the cause of five elements
You are Truth of Truth that is
nothing is beyond you.
What we see is practical Truth
But you are eternal Truth, spiritual
Truth
You lead both, this world and cosmic
world
Truth is your original natural form.

*'Ath sarvagunahpetah Kaalah
paramshobhanah.
Yahyervajanajanmekshe shantakshan
gratarakam.'*

Kaal (time) became beautiful and composite of all virtues. *Kaal* in the phenomenal world is ever engaged in birth-death cycle. At that time moon God was situated in Rohini Nakshatra and in the sky all planets, stars were exhibiting tranquility and placidity.

Kaal is feeling blessed that his master (God) is revealing in him. His blissfulness (*Anand*) was beyond comprehension. *Kaal* became unimaginably beautiful by revealing his all virtues. *Kaal* held inside himself all the virtues of every season and every special time and decorated himself extraordinarily. The spring season breeze with sandal fragrance, the sound of the bird Kokila, the humming of big black bee, the flowers, the flowering in mango orchard, the cleanliness of winter, several flowering plants of cold winter like jasmine, winter flowers, clusters of lotuses of day, lotuses at night, state of trance of early morning, the prayer of the morning, the intention of good work of mid-day, the lunch time hunger, the prayer of evening, the simplicity of night, the joyful and zealous awakening of early morning, the truthfulness of *Satyug, Dev Yagya of Treta Yug*, selfless service of *Dwaparyug* and remembrance of God's name in *Kaliyug*, the treasures of the *Adi Kaal*, the virtues stored; all these attributes made *Kaal* extremely grand.

'Dishah presdurganam nirmaloduganodayam'.

All the ten directions of the Nature became happy; the stars were shinig in the sky as if the blue colored robe was studded with diamonds. In none of the direction there was any kind of dirt. All the guardians of deity of all directions along with their friends were waiting having a kind of bowl in their hands. By the auspicious arrival of bliss all places filled with blissful auspiciousness.

'Mahi mangalbhuyishtha pur gram vrajakara'.

In all the Goldy homes on the earth, city, village and the houses the bliss of divine bliss blissfully started dancing alongwith rivers, ponds, lakes, hills, forests, gardens and all the places.

'Nadyah prasannasalila havada jalroohshriyoh'.

Numerous lotuses bloomed in the lake. The water of rivers became clear and pure. Blooming of lotus in the night means that the entire Nature sacrificing all the bondages started experiencing the bliss and salvation for a few moments, because of incarnation of Lord Krishna who provides salvation. In the forests the leaves of various trees got filled with fragrant flowers of different kinds. The very feel of ever pure and fragrant breeze gave joy and happiness to all.

The full moon of east, filled with full satisfaction, having assumed a flower-like form started waiting in gentle astonishment for the arrival of his beloved God. The clouds holding water were approaching towards ocean with mild blow. In the profound meditative state, the Yogis sitting in precious snow covered caves got infused with Divine bliss and Gods, 'Munis', Yogis, from all directions started praying:

> manifest, manifest
> O! lord appear, appear.
> O! Hari come, come. Then the wonder
> of wonders happened and the oasis
> of *Anand*, '*Satchidananda*' (God)
> appeared. *Jai Ho, Jai Ho* . . . .

> '*Tamadbhutam balakam bhujekshanam*
> *chaturbhujam shadkhagdayudham.*
> *Srivatsalksham galshobhit*
> *kaustubham peetambaram*
> *sandrapayodsobhagam.*'

Devki and Vasudev were wonder struck. Vasudev having experienced the appearance of God was feeling blessed : '*Viditoas Bhagwan Saakshat*'.

O! Lord I have recognized your appearance. Devki in gentle astonishment was looking at God. Devki could see all her previous births. *Anand*—the bliss that Devki was experiencing in having God as child in Krishna was much more than she experienced in God's birth in her previous lives through *Supta Prashani* and *Aditi* and *Kashyap*. *Aditi* and *Kashyap* gave birth to God *Upendra*. With determination and devotion *Devki* and *Vasudev* got the result of their *Sadhana*. The guards of the prison slept, the chains got opened, all the doors of the prison opened. Kansa and his courtiers were under deep sleep and Vasudev keeps the child Krishna in a basket.

'Ishwarah param Krishanh Sachchidanand Vigrah'.

The creator of the entire universe Lord Krishna who is God incarnate proceeds to Gokul—'Krishnastu Bhagvan swayam'. Krishna Bhagvan is going to Gokul. Rescuing saints, killing wickeds and their redemption, establishing *Dharma*, rendering indescribable happiness to devotees, having all attributes, ever existent, without attributes, ever blissful and loving, Sri Radhanayak, Yashod*ananda*m, Nandnandam, Rukmaniraman, world reformer, friend of Sudama and Arjuna, World master—appearance of God is splendid. His grace provides control over sensual organs and merriment and delight.

Yamuna river gave way to Vasudev. Vasudev reached Gokul with child Krishna. Gokul was fully asleep. Aha! The fortunate bed of Yashoda, child Krishna was layed on the bed and Eternal Bliss appeared in Nand's house. *Anand* appeared in Nand's house—*Jai Kanhaiya Lal Ki*.

Inquisitivenss – Desire to Know

The deserving seeker of the Truth, with the Divine Grace of *Sadguru* (the master), attains liberation from life-death cycle by doing unitary worship. The correct methodology for doing unitary worship is given in *Sanatan* (eternal) scriptures, that is, Upanishads. As described in Upanishads the unitary worship is of four kinds. First two are aimed at step *Tat*, and other two are aimed at step *Tvam*. These four kinds of unitary worship are described briefly hereunder:

In the phenomenal world whatever is visible is all Brahman, nothing is other than '*Satchitananda Paramatman*'. Therefore, we should meditate and worship keeping in mind the ONENESS of God in everything.

The living or non-living is Brahman and I am also Brahman (Aham Brahmasmi). Therefore, all over, it is Me and in everything it is Me. In this manner, believing that it is me in everything the *Sadhak* (seeker of Truth) should worship.

The formless God without attributes is altogether free from this perishable, ever-changing and visible world. With this in mind the *Sadhak* should worship.

The one who is formless without attributes, free from this visible, perishable world, the everlasting *Parabrahman* is my Soul. That Soul is me only. Keeping such emotions in mind the *Sadhak* should worship.

In Upanishads, it has been demonstrated and made clear that by performing unitary worship the *Sadhak*(Seeker of the Truth) can attain vastness. Experiencing the God, the *Sadhak* can himself become God. The *Sadhak* is greater than his own material identity. The Upanishad says : *Soakamyat bahusyam prachyeyeti* (Taittriya Upanishad). Thus, Brahman is one and only one but has taken different forms. Therefore, the entire living and non-living world, every nook and cranny is nothing but various forms of Brahman.

Shruti says

> Nectar like Brahman is all over,
> in front there is Brahman, in the back
> there is Brahman, in the right there is
> Brahman in the left there is Brahman,
> upwards and downwards is Brahman.
> Brahman is all pervading. The entire
> world is nothing but Brahman.

The Rishis, the noble persons having pure inner-self, no attachment and fully drenched with Brahman, attain divine wisdom, contentment, straight forwardness and tranquillity. These persons joining themselves with Brahman, ultimately enter into oneness with Brahman.

This entire world in all forms is nothing but *Parambrahman* God, which is the Soul of four quarters and phases and this Soul, is *Parambrahman* God.

This entire world is Brahman beyond doubt. This creation, situation and dynamics (continuous cycle) is from Brahman only. It is, therefore, recommended that the *Sadhak* (Seeker) should timely worship Brahman with still mind.

In the meaning of '*Tat*' this changing world is all Brahman. In accordance with '*Tat*' the changeless form of Brahman could be described as Brahman without attributes, formless, action free, defectless. The Brahman is ever free from this perishable and changing visible world (*Maya*). Whatever is objectively visible in this world as *Maya* is rooted in ignorance.

All that one sees is nothing but infinite, never changing Brahman. With this kind of experience one gets freedom from birth — death cycle and becomes one with Brahman (*Anand*). Yamraj while giving spiritual instructions to Nachiketa says:

> Having known the nectar filled
> Brahman, which is indescribable by
> words, by touch, by smell, and is

> indestructible, everlasting existence
> from the beginning, infinite, beyond
> ego and ultimate Truth, human
> beings get rid of death and birth cycle
> forever.

This Brahman (*Paramatma Tattva*) can only be known by a pure mind. There is no expression but Brahman. Therefore, one who sees this world in different expressions, he is bound by birth and death cycle.

In Mundokupanishad it is mentioned:

> God formless and without
> attributes is neither conceivable
> through eyes, words and other senses,
> nor He can be known, conceived by
> Tapa or action. The eternity (God) can
> just be experienced by a pure *Sadhak*
> having purity of mind, body, *Pran* and
> psyche through consistent meditation
> on Him with purity.

Shruti says:

> *Brahman is the Truth, complete with*
> *wisdom, and infinite.*

After describing the worship of '*Tat*' worship of '*Tvam*' is elaborated.

Whatever we see in the world, living — nonliving is all Brahman and Brahman is Me. Therefore, a person is liable to see the entire world in his

Soul and his Soul in the entire world; meaning thereby that whatever we see is all my own form. The *Sadhak* who practices the above doctrine is liberated from misery, sorrow and attachment and attains the form of *Satchittananda* Brahman. Yogeshvara Bhagvan while explaining to Arjuna, says:

> The Yogi sees all the entities, living—nonliving manifest in the Soul with Oneness of the same consciousness, which is omnipresent and infinite.

Ishavashyoupanishad says:

> The person who sees all creatures in the Soul and understands them as his own Soul, he hates none. How can such a person who sees everybody as his own form hate anyone?

In this way when Oneness prevails in one's mind and he understands everyone as the same Soul, he is free from attachment and sorrow. He comes to understand that the same Brahman pervades in every nook and cranny (living or nonliving). A sacred legend in Chhandyog Upanishad gives a clear cut explanation on this subject:

> Shwetaketu, grandson of Maharishi Arun and son of Rishi

Uddalak enters into *Gurukul* for education. After receiving twelve years of education, Shwetaketu thinking himself to be very intelligent, well versed in giving spiritual discourses and a learned speaker, entered his home discourteously, filled with pride. As soon as he entered his home, he saw his father but did not wish him. The father saw that his son is having ego of knowledge. Then his father told him, Hey Shwetaketu! Hey polite mind! Thinking yourself to be a learned person you are getting immodest. Have you enquired from Acharya about that order by which unheard of, becomes heard? Unthought of, becomes thoughtful, the uncertain becomes certain and the unknown becomes specially known?

Shwetaketu was astonished to hear his father and bowing down to the feet of his father humbly requested him to tell as to what that order is? Rishi Uddalak addressing Shwetaketu said:

My dear son, while knowing the mass of soil, we come to know all the articles made of soil. For example pitcher, various kinds of pots, etc made of soil are nothing but soil. The names and shapes are just to express the items. The Truth is nothing else

> but soil. Similarly, all the items made
> of gold, though called by different
> names are nothing but gold only. The
> truth is gold only.

Having heard his father, Shwetaketu requested his father with reverence to tell him the divine wisdom. O my son! I now tell you this divine wisdom.

Hey Shwetaketu! In the beginning of the creation, the unequalled Truth was God (without a second, supreme) Knowing the inquisitiveness of Shwetaketu, Uddalak rishi explained the subject:

> Just as by churning the curd
> (yogurt), etc, micro fraction, the butter,
> comes out floating at the top. Similarly
> of the food eaten, the micro fraction
> essence makes mind, the water micro
> essence makes '*Pran*' and the fire
> micro fraction makes speech. In fact
> the mind, the *Pran* and the speech and
> their consequential action — reaction
> are due to everlasting eternal
> existence, or only one eternal thing
> that is the Truth (Brahman).

The cause and effect of everything vests in Brahman. The root of everything is the Truth; and is the ultimate shelter. It is due to the Truth that all kinds of forms are disorder of speech, they are for namesake. The Truth is subtle like an atom; it is the Soul of the entire world. Hey, Shwetaketu! You are this Truth. You are *Tattvamasi*.

Shwetaketu wanted to know further. Uddalak Rishi showed him the fruit of *Vat Tree* and said that, this fruit contains thousands of seeds and nothing else. Every seed contains an invisible *'Vat Tree'*. Every seed is capable of becoming a huge tree. And just as the small seed is the base of that invisible tree, similarly the Soul, the subtle Truth, is the base of this material world.

Hey Shwetaketu! I am telling you the Truth. You understand this with full faith, that you are the Truth, the Soul, *Tattvamasi* — You are that Truth.

In this manner Uddalak Rishi explained the Truth and Shwetaketu realised the Ultimate Truth.

Ocean of the Reverential Faith

Faith is the greatest and most auspicious subtle element — *Tattva* of the earth. The credit for the entire protection of the humanity goes to faith. The faith has the greatest contribution for the uninterrupted veneration for mother, father, spiritual masters (*Guru*) and God. A human being is a human being because he thinks, analyses (*munte it manushya*). The power of discrimination makes the human being distinct from the group of other creatures. The power of discrimination comes by knowledge/ wisdom (*Gyan*) and the infinite *Gyan* is God Himself. It acts as equanimity link for visibility of the object of accomplishment. The perceptibility of object gives birth to a state of devotion by creating equanimity in various resources and methods.

Devotion is the mother of concentration. The concentration entirety, *Sadhak* connectivity, and consonance are the arrangement. The concentration is the medium to make one eligible to enter into the unbreakable Soul. Before instructing or preaching, the instructor and preacher concentrates himself to create natural state of involvement with the one to be taught for defining *Tattva*.

It happens when the light of wisdom kindles. It happens when one has faith in the instructor (preacher).

> *'Shradhavan labhte gyanam, gyanam*
> *labhte parama Shanti'*

Faith leads to wisdom (*Gyan*) and wisdom leads to peace. The person, who is devoid of faith, does not get peace and bliss. It is because of ignorance and lack of reverential belief.

Ignorance gives birth to disbelief and the person who lacks reverential belief is generally skeptical. Faith becomes deeper, deeper and firm, when one leaves his own past, misdeeds, interpretations and rules and enters into circumference of infinite eternal simplicity of consciousness of the person. When we come in contact with a great person, a warrior adorned with transcendental valour, a virtuous and kind hearted person, a selfless person and a learned person endowed with wisdom and dignity, in subjection with his honesty a stream of perception (consciousness), boundless belief, natural honor and reverential feelings appear. On hearing their words; pure perception of belief takes birth in our hearts for sacred verses, pilgrimage, learned persons, *Yagya*, spiritual masters (*Guru*), yogis, great persons and we become respectful towards all elements. Faith is the real spring of *Dharma* and culture. On the strength of reverential belief the entire world is stable in the form of Universe.

Srimad Bhagvad Gita enunciates that the charity, philanthropy, *Yagya* (sacrifice), ascetic fervor etc, without faith, reverence and veneration are all false and do not bear fruit (*ashraddh yahutam danam na ch tatpretya no ih*). Lord Krishna says: to get closer to God, faith is an essentiality. *Shrdhadhanva matpsam bhaktosteyateev mein priya:*

The devotee who remembers Me with great faith, he gets My utmost love.

There is a deep psychological mystery, confering well being is placed in respectful greeting of an honorable and venerable person. When we touch the feet of venerable person our ego gets dissolved and our consciousness becomes expansive. Bowing down the head in the lotus feet of the lord in the temple destroys ego. It leads to getting oneself into expansive vision of boundless *Tattva*. For a person offering respectful greetings Bhagvan Manu expressed His good feelings-

'*Abhivadamsheelasyanityamyashobalam*; meaning thereby, that the age, education (knowledge), glory and strength of such a person grow together. Faith inspires intellect towards the right path. Intellect without faith (reverence) drags towards doubt, restlessness, confusion and dejection. Thus, *Sat-Chit-Anand* (existence — knowledge — bliss), is achieved through the medium of reverential attitude. Arguments and intellect cannot even touch the level that is attainable through faith. In disappearance (omission) of faith, *Dharma* and culture also disappear. In Vedanta, about faith it is said—'*Gurupadshti Vedantvakyshu vishvash*' i.e. the belief in the words of spiritual masters (*Guru*) and Shashtra, *Dharma* and scriptures is called reverential faith. '*Shraddhaya satyen yagyen swargan lokan jayati*—Eternal Brahman. By reverential faith the host devotee can win over heaven.

> *Shaddhaya deva devattvamashnute*
> *Shadda pratishtha lokasya lokasya Devi.*
> *. . . . Ishan Devi bhuvhasya adhipathi.*

Through these sacred words (Mantra), reverential faith has been given lavish praise, because it takes one close to godliness, to the ruler of all the *Lokas*, to the preserver and nourisher of the world. Tripur—mystery has described faith as affectionate mother.

It has also been mentioned that when *Jiva* is filled with impurity and ego, his prosperity, bliss and state of happiness vanishes.

In Markandey Puran, Durga (Goddess of power and strength) has been constantly worshiped as reverential faith. (*Yadevi sarvabhuteshu shraddha rupen sansisthta, namastasyey namastasyey namastasyey namoh namah*).

Srimad Bhagvad Gita has described faith in three forms: *Sattavic, Rajsic* and *Tamas*ic. Selfless disposition of faith in paternal ancestors, teachers and spiritual masters (*Guru*) is *Sattavic* faith. With impure mind, just as show of business, is artificial faith and it is called *Tamsik* faith, whereas, faith with the desire of pleasure and wealth is called as *Rajasic* faith.

Ignorance is the mother of ego, which is very powerful. Stronger the ego, weaker is the faith. As the ego diminishes, the reverential faith takes its place. We become, what we think and what we absorb and express through our senses. It is therefore warranted that we should feel goodness to our body, mind and intellect.

Soliciting worthiness from forgetfulness, warding off, and recollection is mentioned. Such worthiness is achievable by thinking all the time about the blissful kingdom of the Soul. Discriminating power of real and unreal, coordination of resources and their right use, and devotional worship of the idol (God) renders crop of sainthood. Looking into the vices of others is a seizing resource.

Accepting the duty/ obligation and finishing the left over is the guide for purity of vision. Pure vision makes pure mind. The reflection of reverential faith in the mind makes one filled with Brahman. A continuous flow of *Anand* (bliss) incarnates.

Sanatan Tattva—Eternal Reality

I n the *Shashtras* (Indian Scriptures), the word *Dharma* has invariably been used at all places. No adjective has been used at all. No adjective has been used to qualify *Dharma*. Use of any adjective for infinite thing confines it to a limited boundary. For example the word flower indicates all flowers of the world/universe. Similarly by saying *Dharma*, it represents all the *Dharma*s of the world—Universe. By saying Jain *Dharma*, Budh *Dharma* etc, only a part of *Dharma* comes into the mind. Though in scriptures—Manuscript, Mahabharat—*Eshah Dharmah Sanatanoh* has been added at some places, with the word *Dharma*. But addition of word *Sanatan* does not limit the meaning of *Dharma*; rather it has added to its glory. This means this word *Dharma* is *Sanatan* (eternal).

Dharma is derived from *Dhratra* – meaning thereby that *Dharma* holds everything or by which all the things in world are held and protected.
Narayan Upanishad says

> The entire world rests on *Dharma*.
> *Dharma* is the root of existence.
> Maharishi Vedavyas has written – it
> preserves and maintains, that is
> why it is called *Dharma*. *Dharma*
> holds, preserves and maintains
> people. Which is capable of holding,
> preserving and maintaining is called
> *Dharma*. God's eternal power and
> wish, which holds the entire world,
> is called *Dharma*. God is omnipresent.
> His power pervades in all the objects.
> The five elements (aakash, air, water,
> earth and fire) and sun, moon, stars,
> rivers, mountains, etc all objects are
> resting in their respective places
> due to His power. In absence of His
> power the entire existence becomes
> catastrophic. If the earth did not have
> holding power, then it would have got
> burnt or blown away like air. Similarly
> in the absence of the holding power of
> *Dharma*, no object in the world could
> have rested in the world in its place.

It is because of the *Dharma*, fire burns, sun gives heat and *Indra*, air and *Yam* are bound to do their respective work. As the power of the king is spread through the entire kingdom, the eternal power of *Dharma* holds, preserves and maintains the entire universe. This is the undistinguished feature of our *Dharma* as enunciated in our Vedic scriptures. All the *Dharma*s of the world get absorbed in the expansive feature of this Universal *Dharma*. No other *Dharma* has this type of characteristic.

Scriptures (Shashtras) tell us about the other feature of *Dharma*-

Dharma provides improvements, ascendance and salvation. Maharishi Vedavyas has written in Mahabharat-

By practicing *Dharma* all the creatures (*Jiva*), through the succession, reach ultimate goal of becoming one with the source. All the creatures (*Jiva*) taking birth at the lowest level of nature, gradually improve and ascend; and ultimately become one with Brahman and get rid of three gunas — *Sattva, Raj, Tam* in equal proportion. When *Rajaguna* is dominant, the creation of *Rajoguna* is lifeless creation. It creates only five elements (earth, water, fire, air and aakash). *Sattvaguna* is illuminated, that is why it possesses the power to absorb the reflection of *Chetana* (eternal power of life). The dominance of *Sattvaguna* creates life nature. Due to reflection of Brahman in the life, it is known as *Jiva* and further development of power to act and gain knowledge takes place.

At first, *Sattvaguna* is present in the state of vegetable kingdom — such as trees, creepers plants etc. *Jiva* (life) undergoes nearly two million years of succession in this state of life. Thereafter

Jiva (life) enters into the form of insects. For one million years *Jiva* (life) takes birth as birds, fish etc. This category is known as egg born creatures and *Jiva* lives in this category of creatures for nearly two million years—Subsequently, in succession:

Jiva(life) proceeds to viviparous creatures. After living nearly three and a half million years as viviparous creatures, *Jiva* (life) takes birth as human being. The succession of *Jiva* (life) in this manner remains unbroken under the influence of the power of *Dharma* only. This phenomenon of our *Dharma* is universally applicable in all the creatures including human being. No religion is excluded by this *Dharma*. What is our duty towards *Dharma*? The action that helps such succession of improvement and ascent develops *Sattvguna,* that is *Dharma*. Our Shashtras (scriptures) say that *Yagya*, philanthropy, charity, prayers, sharing—caring with those who are less lucky, welcoming guest with honor, etc help the above process of improvement.

Therefore, for the mind of human being these are a great inspirational strength. The strength that we get by following spiritual models, no other model can provide. As far as the history of man is concerned, the strength of *Dharma* is concerned; the strengths of *Dharma* are not dead. The lives of those persons, who with their spiritual fire, illuminate others lives, always emerge through the platform of spirituality. The source of their inspirational strength has always been *Dharma*. *Dharma* is greatest inspirational power for the

227

visibility of infinite strength, which is the nature of every human being and his birth right.

Character building and acquisition of eternal auspiciousness (Shiv) and greatness are the highest order of inspirational power to obtain peace in the world and oneself. As the human mind develops, spiritual steps also expand. Preservation of basics of *Dharma* is very important to carry the grandeur and beauty of this creation. When we stand on the real spiritual and expansive platform, then and only then, *Dharma* will come to reality. It will become a part of our life. It will be in every fibre of the society.

Its power of eternal auspiciousness will increase manifold — become infinite. Among the powers/ strengths that have helped human beings in making their destiny and are helping in the present, *Dharma* has been and is the greatest. The human being who is highly educated and disciplined, no doubt gets joy in art, science, philosophy; but spirituality occupies the greatest state of happiness. Spirituality being infinite in the greatest state, those who take it into their hearts, achieve peace, happiness, and purity of the highest order which is permanent. Therefore this essence of *Dharma* must be practiced in daily life.

Shiv *Tattva*

The present era is an era intensely devoid of faith and belief, respect and consideration and regard. In the entire world there is strife, anarchy, restlessness and anxiety. In the present context, it is necessary to visit spiritual '*Tattva*', so as to develop humanity, peace, love and make our life happy. The base of spiritual *Tattva* is Shiv *Tattva*. Shiv means auspicious and eternal (everlasting). If we know what is Shiv, then the mystics about the existence of this world reveal themselves.

'*Shete tishthati sawa jagat yasmin sah shambhuh vikarrahitah*'. Where the entire world is resting, and the *Tattva* which is responsible and possesses the right is Shiv *Tattva* — Lord Shiv is full of compassion, eternal (everlasting), and the Truth and blissful. Lord Shiv is without beginning or end. He is the witness of the world, beginning or end. He is the witness of every era of the world (*satya, treta, dvapara and kali*). He is eternal, sovereign, universal, immortal Truth.

Hey Shiv! I know, I do not have any knowledge. I am ignorant. I am not capable of expressing your wholeness. Even Brahman and other's are not capable of comprehending your eternity. It is, therefore beyond my comprehension to know your wholeness.

The causal knowledge is an obstacle for a human being to recognize his 'own self'. Shiv is absolutely free from such ignorance (causal knowledge). Lord Shiv is free and beyond the entire world, individuality, worldly affairs and entanglements, development and expansion, toils of the world. That's why Lord Shiv is called as '*Digamber*' (one who has space as clothing). *Digamber* means free from all covering.

Lord Shiv is all pervasive and powerful and smeared with ash. The actions performed by intellect and mind, accumulate as deeds performed in earlier births and become the cause of bondage. Having achieved Brahman knowledge all these actions are destroyed and there is no rebirth, because like the ash they become little.

The different objects (items) when reduced to ashes look alike. Thus the ash illustrates oneness of all objects.

The significance of matted hair of Lord Shiv is that, '*Har*' or direct God is the resting place of those beings that have attained freedom from rebirth. The matted hair is like '*Vat-Vraksh*' Like matted hair of Lord Shiv, *Vedanta, Sankhya* and Yoga are the three ornaments of '*Vat-Vraksh*'

The third eye of Lord Shiv signifies:

> Shankara, like moon provides
> bliss of the universe, like the sun is the
> destroyer of *Tamas* (dullness/ laziness)
> and like fire destroys vices, attachment
> and envy. That's why he is worshipped
> as *Trinetra (Chandrasuryagninayam)*.

The garland of snakes in the neck of Lord of Spirit (Shiv) signifies:

> Yogis live on air, like snakes do
> and they stay in caves of the hills.
> As the snakes live in isolation with
> brevity, they are very dear to Lord
> Shiv and they are ornaments of his
> body. That is why Lord Shiv is also
> known as one who maintains snakes.

Trishul (trident of Lord Shiv) expresses number of facts of life. Peace is the result of practicing *Yam – Niyam*, not allowing the mind, thought and behavior to take form and moderation of conduct.

The desire for renunciation of objects of enjoyment and their shortage, the richness of intellect, realization or discrimination of true and false, through which the oneness of Soul and ego comes and goes, produces peace. These three means are capable of piercing through the ignorance and the deeds performed out of ignorance; and therefore they symbolize the three blades of the Trident of Lord Shiv (*Trishul*). With the Trishul Lord Shiv destroys *Sattva, Raj and Tam gunas.* He also destroys gross, subtle and named body, which acts under the influence of the three gunas. Giving affirmation to false *Tattva* He generates detachment in it. This is the significance of the possession of the Trident(Trishul).

Lord Shiv is free from all kind of impurities and bondage (atomic, molecular, action, *Maya*, nature, intellect, ego, prestige, honor, money, sense organ, essential elements etc.)

Shiv, with immeasurable *Tejas* (brilliance) is not bound by time, art, knowledge, destiny, attachment and envy. He is actionless and free from the results thereof. Neither is he connected to desires, nor to the outcome. He is also free from past, present and future. He is neither doer nor cause or effect. He has no beginning and no duty. He has neither any friend nor any foe, neither any controller nor motivator, neither any husband nor any master (*Guru*) or savior and protector. He is unparalleled, how can He be described in words? He neither takes birth nor dies. Nothing is essential or non essential for Him. There is neither any rule nor any restriction for Him. Neither bondage, nor freedom (salvation); inauspicious shortcomings do not touch Him. But He possesses all kinds of auspicious attributes. Shiv is God by Himself.

Shiv being present all over, is always stable without losing His nature; and therefore he is called (an epithet of Shiv) that is motionless. The entire world is under the control of Shiv. Lord Shiv is in all forms. A person who understands Lord Shiv's mystics is devoid of all attachments.

Omnipresent – All Pervading

Sri Vishnu Bhagvan (Lord), the purest existence (Being), complete with all the virtuous attributes, the authority of the three *Lokas*, the everlasting eternal existence, the real Truth, the beginning of the beginning and beginning before beginning . . . . is all pervading with perfect equanimity.

> *Om mangalam bhagvan Vishnu*
> *mangalam garunadhvajah,*
> *Mangalam Pundreekaksho*
> *mangalayayatno Hari.*

In Vedas and Puranas, etc He is called as the Truth, the Ultimate Reality, never changing existence (Being); The Vedic learned persons who are always thinking of Brahman, address this purest existence (Being) as *Indra, Mittra, Varuna,*

Agni, Yam, Matrishva, Divine, Suparn, Gurutmah, etc.

These are various names of the Supreme Consciousness, Vishnu, representing oneness, i.e. the presence of one and the same *Tattva* in every nook and cranny — living or non-living. In various deities Sri Vishnu is present as the Truth/ *Tattva*. The meaning of the Truth is — that which does not change under any condition, always remains the same. Theists call this unchanging *Tattva* (the Ultimate Reality — The Truth), Brahman. Those who have the realization of the Brahman, pray: *'Asto ma sadgamya'* (from unreal, lead me to the Truth).

> *Vigyansarthriya istu manah*
> *pragrahavannarsh*
> *Soadhvanah parmapnoti tadvishno param*
> *padam.*

Vishnu means omnipresent; which is present everywhere.

Learned Vedantic persons have presented their commentary according to their own thinking.

1. *Kaushitki*: One who is present in all is Vishnu.
2. *Sayhacharya*: Vishnu is omnipresent with 'Vish'
3. Oldenburg: In the sense of expansive effort, endeavor, industry (vi+snu) is Vishnu.

4. Bloomfield: In the sense of being supremely placed (Supreme consciousness) (Vi+ nu) is Vishnu.
5. Mcdonnel: Vish means being industrious, and in the meaning of businessman (vish+ nu) is Vishnu.
6. *Dayanand Saraswati*: Born from all pervading elements (viz, earth, water, fire, air, aakash) ' Vish', Vishnu means omnipresent.

It clearly proves that learned persons are of the same view; because omnipresence is synonymous to continuous motion; and getting into every nook and cranny, to be ascending, to be industrious etc, also represents continuous motion. Thus, meaning of Vishnu being omnipresent is concordantly proven.

In Vedantic principles Vishnu is understood as formless, everlasting energy. Vedantic commentators have explained Vishnu as Supreme Consciousness (God), all pervading, omnipresent Brahman. Vishnu is formless and in form also; with attributes and without attributes as well. Vishnu is *Para Brahman*. It is not possible to describe His greatness, grandeur and glory by any creature of nature. He is beyond description by mind, intellect or words. Vedas also stop after saying Neti, Neti, Neti . . . . (not this, not this, not this . . . .).

Vishnonum kam viryani pravocham, ya
parthivani vimse rajansi, Yo askabhaya
dutturun sadhasyam vichakramanastrey
dhorugayah vishnavetva.

(Yajur Veda)

Vishnonum kam virjani pravocham, ya
parthivani vimse rajansi,
Yo askabhaya dutturum sadhasyam
vichakramanastrey dhorngayah.

(Rig Veda, Atharva Veda)

Who can be capable of describing the infinite power and valor of Shri Vishnu? Sri Vishnu has created numerous Universes with His Yogmaya power, Nature, in the grandeur and glory of ONENESS.

Sri Vishnu is of infinite glory. This never changing *Tattva* is called the Truth/ Para Brahman,

'Param Akshar Vishnu' (unperishable), ever — existent, the greatest of the greatest. He has created place of Nirvana. Sri Vishnu's glory and grandeur cannot be described. The Truth, the everlasting *Tattva*, *ParaBrahman*, Vishnu all are synonymous words. They all represent one *Tattva*, and are, therefore, one and the same. This further establishes the principle that everlasting, ever existent Truth is Vishnu from the beginning of the beginning and before beginning of the beginning . . . . He is always filled with ONENSS.

Vishnu is complete in all respects and represents the fourth state of the Soul in which the Soul has become one with the Supreme spirit. Vishnu is ' Param Akashar Para Brahman'.

O Lord! You are the Soul of mind like *Mansarovar* of munis and Shiv, and for whom the yogis perform yoga denunciating their anger, attachment, ego, greed. You are everlasting, imperishable, omnipresent Brahman, *Chidananda*, without attributes and with attributes. It is not possible to know you by mind, intellect or word. Only you are the Being—The Truth can be inferred.

The Soul is Immortal

Maharshi Yagyavalkya decided to leave family life and go for complete renunciation. He called both his wives and equally divided his property into two parts. His first wife Katyayani accepted her share of the property; and thus did not pose any obstacle in renunciation; but the second wife Maittrayee said—Oh Maharshi! what good fortune (virtues, auspiciousness, prosperity), the property that you are giving me, will bring to my life? Can it provide the elixir of everlasting *Tattva*? Can I be elixir like blissful by getting the grandeur and majesty of whole world? Maharshi was pleased with these beautiful words of Maittrayee and said: 'Maittrayee you are blessed, praiseworthy and virtuous'.

Money, luxuries and power are not capable of providing the elixir *Tattva*. Perishable material things keep one away from the supreme *Tattva*. Maittrayee said I want the knowledge of elixir

Tattva, never changing *Tattva*, the Truth and eternal *Tattva*. Hearing this, Yagyavalkya said—Maittrayee you are blessed and virtuous. Your inquisitiveness to know the Truth is great and I am much impressed.

Hey Maittrayee! The purpose of life is—'love for all'. The Soul alone is worth experiencing, listening, thinking and meditating upon. Inquisitiveness to know, listen, experience, think and meditate provides the wisdom (*Gyan*).

This *Atman* without form, without defect (changeless), everlasting science of '*Anand*' (bliss) is '*Parabrahman Parmatma*' i.e. indistinctive, Brahman, which is devoid of this ever—changing and perishable vision of phenomenal world, full of '*Maya*'(the objective scenes that actually do not have permanence but seem to exist). The Brahman is our Soul. Knowing of the oneness of our Brahman, one becomes Brahman.

Shruti says:

> One who is desireless and self
> educating about Brahman does not
> feel lifeless; he being Brahman attains
> Brahman.

Once, king Janak performed a big *Yagya*. The King invited many learned persons and arranged for spiritual discourses. After the completion of the *Yagya*, king Janak announced that the one who has attained the knowledge of Brahman will get ten thousand cows studded with gold in their horns as gift, which he can carry to his *Ashram* (place of living). All the invited learned persons looked at each other.

Yagyavalkya was also present among them. He pointed towards his disciples to take away all the cows to the *Ashram*. His disciples took away all the cows to the *Ashram*. The other learned persons present questioned as to how you are Brahmanisht (one who has the knowledge of Bhahman and always thinks of Brahman). Yagyavalkya gave solutions to all the questions put forth by Ashraval, Artabhag and Bhujya.

Having heard the deeply resolved knowledge of Maharishi Yagyavalkya, Chakrayan Ushashta asked Maharishi Yagyavalkya, Hey Yagyavalkya! Elaborate about the directly visible Brahman and immortal Soul.

Yagyavalkya said as follows:

It is the Soul that is immortal. Ushashta enquired what this immortal Soul is? Yagyavalkya replied — It is the immortal Soul that acts through *Pran*. Ushashta further enquired — What is immortal? Yagyavalkya said — Your Soul is immortal. You cannot see the witness (subject) of that sight, you cannot hear the listener of the sense of hearing, you cannot think over the thought of the mind. You cannot know the knower of the known. Only your Soul is immortal, what is different from Soul is all mortal. The phenomenal world is mortal and

only you, that is, only your Soul is
immortal.

Having learnt this, Ushashta Chakrayan
achieved tranquillity. Thereafter, Kaushitkeya
Kahol enquired — What is this immortal?
Yagyavalkya said — the immortal is that which
is beyond hunger, thirst, sorrow, attachment,
infirmity and death. It is your Soul that is
immortal.

Kaushitkeya achieved tranquillity. Then
Yagyavalkya, explaining to Arunya Uddalak,
said — the one who resides in the earth but the
earth is ignorant about Him, the one whose body
is the earth and who regulates the earth, He is your
Soul; the Soul is knower of the inner thoughts.

The Soul is invisible but knower of the visible,
the Soul is the listener, and the Soul is not the
object but the sensor of the object. The Soul is the
knower of the known. Your Soul is the knower of
the known. Your Soul is the knower of the inner
thoughts. Your Soul is immortal nectar. Anything
other than the Soul is mortal and perishable.

Having heard this Aruni also achieved
tranquillity. Like this, all the learned persons
assembled in the *Yagya* organised by King Janak
became quiet and achieved tranquillity.

Vrahdaranyak Upanishad explains this in a
simple way :

He is the greatest unborn, indestructible
Soul, everlasting nectar, fearless and Brahman.
Certainly Brahman is fearless and one who knows
this by experience becomes fearless Brahman.

Nothing different from your '*Own Self*'. Soul is all pervading. It is oneness. The *Sadhak*as who perform worship having this in mind attain Brahman. The result of worshipping God is God.

Bhagvan Krishna explains to Arjuna — Many *Sadhak*s see God in their heart through subtle and pure mind and many see God via *Gyanyoga* (wisdom) and many see God through *Karmyoga* (action). All attain Brahman. Gita, Upanishad and many other scriptures present different methods of *Sadhana* and worship but the result of all of them is the same, that is attainment of Brahman. This leads to the 'Universality of Oneness'.

Practicing *Dharma*

Dharma Tattva (the real state of righteousness) is the regulating *Tattva* (supreme spirit) of life. In the absence of *Dharma*, life is non-existent. The nourishing element of life is *Dharma*. 'Driyate Dharma ityaahuh sa evam parmah prabhuh' — meaning thereby that what is to be held, maintained and preserved is *Dharma*. What is Sin — Righteousness, Wisdom — Ignorance, Beautiful — Ugly?

In summary, what is good and bad? *Dharma* is *Sanatan*, (eternal) by which the entire universe (the three worlds — heaven, earth and ether regions) is held and sustained. Not only the entire universe/world but that which can be counted in them, is held, sustained, preserved and controlled by *Dharma*. *Dharma Tattva* is the conductor/operator of the universal structure. Man is considered superior to other creatures, as he is capable of acquiring knowledge/ wisdom of

Dharma. Only human body is suitable to perform *Dharma Sadhana* (practice *Dharma*).

Therefore, human being can go forward for *Sadhana* to achieve wisdom of *Dharma* and with a keen desire he can easily achieve success in *Dharma Sadhana*. But the other creatures cannot do so. Nevertheless, the other creatures are also held and sustained by *Dharma*. Human being is blessed with freedom of choice.

Other creatures are dependent on Nature. Western scientists (Herbert Spencer and others) say that according to sequential turning (succession) point of view, a tiny particle of sand can change into a big hill or it can even become human being and can diffuse the infinite light of wisdom. It is absolutely correct; the *Dharma* of the particle of sand attracts it towards law of ascending path, and due to law of sequential turning or improvements, birth after birth converts it into the form of human being. What else can be so wondrous? The successive progress of the particle of sand is based on *Dharma* of Nature. But the man being blessed with mind and choice, his keen desire alone can make him understand *Dharma*, and take him to the greatest height of spirituality, that is self—realization.

However, it cannot be taken for granted that a human being will automatically get *Dharma Gyan*. Many people are neither conversant with what is *Dharma*, nor are they keen to know about *Dharma*, nor do they perform any *Sadhana* (practice) to understand *Dharma*. Most people work for self pleasure and comforts and remain busy for the same throughout life. Despite this *Dharma* exists, whether they follow or not.

It is *Dharma* alone that makes one climb the ladder of improvement. It is applicable to all tiny particles of sand, birds and animals. It is based on natural sequential turning (succession). Man is endowed with knowledge of *Dharma* and he possesses the energy (power) to practice and apply. He has self dependence quality. That is why man is considered to be the best (most excellent) among all the creatures. Those who follow the *Dharma* (humanity) are eligible to be called human being. Those who are just engaged in eating, sleeping and are fearful, are just like animals disguised in human body. Therefore, the prime duty of man is to get knowledge of *Dharma*. By the grace of God, man has been endowed with the power through which he can ascend to the highest peak of improvement, since he has been given the power to do *Sadhana* (practice) for attaining knowledge of *Dharma*. That power is knowledge of *Dharma*. To practice *Dharma* and develop natural humanity is the prime duty of all human beings. However, humanity is not the ultimate peak. Following *Dharma*, man should try to achieve godliness and then proceed to shelter in Brahman; so that beatific state of communion of the Soul with the divine being (Brahman) is attained. Man has such eternal energy (power).

It is because of this latent energy that man is the best. Practicing mental reflection of latent energy, man attains beatific state of communion with Brahman. This is called *Dharma* and practicing the same is known as *Dharma Sadhana*. Man knows all this, but still he is engaged in the visible world to get pleasure, joy, happiness and comfort. He is engrossed in endless desires. That's why he is surrounded by sorrow and miseries all along. How can he be happy? Where is happiness? Following and practicing inner wisdom and *Dharma* can provide supreme satisfaction. By *Dharma* one can attain full alertness of senses and satisfaction to get coordinated accomplishment.

Everyone desires for happiness but the happiness takes birth from *Dharma*. Therefore, practicing *Dharma* brings happiness. The happiness derived from outer material world is not permanent. The material happiness is left behind after death of the body. Therefore, it is of little use. Only *Dharma* gives company. It is therefore, the duty of man to recourse and plan to get rid of bondage of attachment and achieve 'self realisation'. To be born as human being is most difficult and precious. Therefore, self improvement is the objective of man. *Dharma* is the recourse for the same. There could be no other friend but *Dharma*. The special thing is that our Soul is the part of Supreme Soul (Brahman). Man is always busy in search of happiness but due to ignorance he is unable to get permanent happiness, despite his wish. For want of happiness people are engrossed in senses that attract outer world (from colour, smell, taste, touch, money). It is like a mirage. There is sorrow, misery and dissatisfaction in the material things.

Therefore, in comparison to *Brahmananda* (Permanent happiness) all other sources of happiness are mean. Brahman is omnipresent — all pervading. Awareness (Being) and body are clear-cut and Her existence is also clear — cut. Body is also clear-cut and visible but we are unable to catch the point of separateness. Once we get it, we will get the source of permanent happiness. Temporary things can give temporary happiness. *Gyan* (knowledge) of everlasting *Tattva* (Brahman) can provide permanent happiness.

God-Like State – GODLY BEHAVIOUR

As soon as *Jiva* looks at the visible world, he clearly gets the glimpses of two opposite streaks of path, which are called *Praiya* and *Shraiya*, that is dear and auspicious, respectively. *Praiya* path is comparatively easier and attractive from materialistic point of view. Common men follow it, despite the fact that the result is sorrow and misery. Followers of *Shraiya* path are rare. Those who have a balanced mind are able to choose *Shraiya* path. To focus the state and behavior of mind on *Shraiya* path, is as difficult as to divert small streams of water in opposite direction by embankment. Even a small hole is sufficient to breach the dam and destroy the resource. From the very beginning, the Indian philosophers and thinkers have pronounced the *Gyan (knowledge)*, Action and Devotion Yoga as the resources;

considering the main object/ goal of human being is to attain salvation.

Bhagvan Krishna has described these resources to His close associate Udhava as under:

Gyan, Devotion and Action Yoga are the resources for the welfare of human being, and there is definitely no other resource.

Gyan Yoga

Actions performed by all the senses, body and mind devoid of the ego of doing the action, and keeping unitary feeling with omnipresent Brahman is known as *Gyan* Yoga.

Bhishma, while explaining to Yudhishthar, highlighted the expressions of Bhagvan Vedavyas on the importance of *Gyanyoga* in the following words-

As consequences of actions performed, the result appears as pleasure and sorrow, birth and death. But by *Gyan* the *Sadhak* achieves that extraordinarily difficult road of salvation, which makes him free from sorrow and provides him everlasting peace and happiness.

The right to get *Gyan* is only for the *Sadhak* who has control over his senses and practices with full faith, the preaching of learned persons (*Tattva Gyani* — one who understands the Truth, i.e. omnipresence of never changing Brahman). As soon as one comes to know Self, he at once attains permanent happiness and peace. In fact knowledge about Self is the state of *Ananda* or realization of real state of peace.

Karamyoga

Relinquishing the result of *Karamyoga* (action) and attachments of actions, as divine order of equanimity, is known as desireless *Karamyoga*. This is also called equanimity yoga. Sri Krishna told Arjuna about *Karamyoga* as under:

Hey Arjuna! Fix yourself in the state of Karmyoga, relinquishing all attachments and keeping equality in success and failure, perform actions; because evenness of mind is Yoga; meaning thereby to keep the feeling of equanimity towards all non-living and living beings. Every nook and cranny is nothing but Brahman. Keeping this feeling in mind performance of action as an inspiration of Brahman without selfishness, attachment, pride and thought of success or failure, is the key of *Karamyoga*.

Perfect equanimity is the highest Yoga. Experiencing sorrow and joy, prosperity and poverty, accomplishment and non-accomplishment, blame and praise with equality is Yoga. To get rid of detachment from the outcome of the action.

Sri Krishna tells Arjuna that, 'your right is restricted to perform your duty only'. The result is a thing that is always beyond your competence. Never be greedy for the results. Inaction is also not warranted, continue to act. This is the highest counsel of Gita. This is the highest *Gyan* (knowledge) enunciated in Gita with regard to detachment. The doer is meant for performing action, that is, it exists in the present. The

251

attachment towards the result, which is not seen immediately, is a hidden form of greed, which is in no way auspicious.

A peasant is to do work in his field and sow suitable seeds. To get the crop according to his wish is beyond his competence.

> *'Twadeeyam vastu Govindam tubhyameva samarpaye'*-

Govinda (Sri Krishna), these are your things and we offer them to Thou (we should have this feeling in our mind all the time).

Sow the seeds in the field. It is good not to have any feeling of greed and pride in the mind. The accomplishment of the results is not solely based on our labor but is also influenced by daily and physical powers. One who has attachment with results is likely to become actionless, lazy and dull, in case he does not get the results to his expectations. Any delay or failure may affect him seriously. Many *Sadhak*s give up their efforts and actions on account of sorrow or bondage, which is not good for them. Sri Krishna told Arjuna that you should think that you are doer of the action. You have to continuously work without attachment.

This is the main expounded subject of Srimad Bhagvad Gita. In the third chapter of Gita, Sri Krishna teaches *Karamyoga* to Arjuna: By nature human beings belong to two kinds of situations, one is introspective and other is extrovert. Persons endowed with the introspective brilliance, keeping the world and material pleasures away engage themselves for ever in the development of their inner self. This is known as *Gyanyoga path or Sanyasa* path to escape rebirth. The extrovert person getting attached to worldly and material pleasures remains busy in numerous worldly actions and this is called *Karmayogi* or inclinative path. In fact both these paths are complementary to each other, because no one can be wholly introspective or wholly extrovert.

Generally all human beings are introspective in small fractions and extrovert in large proportion. Sri Krishna says that working without personal interest is better and easier than *Gyan path.* Nevertheless, saying so is easier than practicing in daily life. Nobody can avoid doing action even for a moment. Under the influence of obvious attributes of nature, everyone has to perform one or the other action. It is impossible to escape action, while we are living. Even after becoming a recluse, some effort is to be done for food for hunger and thirst. *Karma path* is easier for realization of Brahman.

Bhaktiyoga

Bhaktiyoga (worship and devotion): Bhakti is defined as to worship the lotus feet of God with purity and piousness and experience of faith and love without attachment and desire for worldly things. Absence of materialistic fancy and eagerness for the desire and pleasure of senses are an essential aspect for a devotee;

because love eradicates duality forever. In the presence of worldliness, it is not possible to attain transcendental state (unearthly state). Next, the greater the concentration and undivided love the higher is the elevation. Unification with God through undivided worship and devotion is called *Bhaktiyoga*.

Lord Krishna says that — *Bhaktiyoga* is continuous remembrance of God (Vasudev) with greatest love and faith. Absence of selfishness and pride (ego) is essence of *Bhaktiyoga*. As all the rivers, when merged with the ocean, become ocean, similarly all paths leads to same destination (realization of omnipresence of Brahman i.e. Oneness). The *Sadhak*s should follow the path told by *Guru* (the spiritual master), the path enunciated in scriptures (*Shastras*) and the path followed by noble persons.

Sesasai

'Vishnu reclining on sesa-a — thousand headed snake regarded as symbol of Eternity on which Vishnu sleeps throughout period of dissolution of the world.'

> *Vasdembol vpara veda vasudev para makhah,*
> *Vasudevpara yoga Vasudevpara kriya,*
> *Vasudevparama gyanam Vasudevparam tapah,*
> *Vasudevparo dharmo Vashdevpara gatih.*

All the Shashtras (scriptures) enunciate that Bhagvan Vasudev grants release from rebirth in the world; chanting Bhagvan Vasudev — *Om Namo Bhagvate Vasudevay*, has such a power. Vedas groups, *Yagya*, wisdom, *tapasaya* etc, all are characterized by Bhagvan Vasudev. All works of *Dharma* have the conclusion (end) in Bhagvan Vasudev.

In the beginning of the creation Bhagvan desired to create *Lokas* (Universes, cosmological regions). This desire led Him to take birth in the form of *Purush* (man) from the greatest authority (omnipotence). Ten senses, a mind, five elements and sixteen arts. Yogis with their divine vision see the *Purush* form of Bhagwan Vishnu. This form of Bhagvan Vishnu having thousands of feet, arms and mouths is extraordinarily astonishing and is of distinguishing characteristics of thousands of heads, thousands of ears, thousands of eyes and thousands of noses.

This form of Bhagvan Vishnu is rapturous and joyful with thousands of delightful crowns, clothes, ear-rings etc. This *Purush* form of Bhagvan is called *Narayan* and it is the never ending treasure of His several incarnations. All incarnations appear from this *Purush* form. The creations of all kinds of creatures in the world including man take place from *Purush*. As the attributes of Bhagvan are innumerable, so are His names. His every name represents His attributes and all these names are of the same Bhagvan Vishnu. He is only one and all pervading God — omnipresent, omnipotent and omniscient.

As He is the creator of this world, His one name is Brahma' — *Bhookhilam jagannirmanen brahanti vardhyati sah Brahma.*

Due to His being omnipresent and all pervading He is called 'Vishnu' — *Vevisht vyapanotic characharam jagat sa Vishnuh*. He also looks after the welfare of this phenomenal world. That is why His name is 'Shiv' In the essence, all these names, irrespective of expression and countries are of one and the same God. He is one and only one (there is no duality). It is ONENESS. These are some of the aspects of names and attributes of God.

Now let us look at the aspects of worshipping God. People worship God in different ways — some worship Shiv, some worship Vishnu, some worship Goddess Durga, some worship spirit. In this manner, different persons worship differently and at times, they talk against each other looking seriously at their methods of worshipping, which reveal that their works are nothing but ignorance.

In Gita, Bhagvan Krishna has said, while worshipping different Gods, people worship Me only i.e. Supreme God Vishnu; the medium being different.

> *Yeapyany devata bhakta yajantey*
> *shraddhayanvitah,*
> *Teapi mamev kaunteya japantic*
> *vidhipurvakam.*

Hey Arjuna! Though the men worship different Gods, but in fact they do worship Me only. However their worship is with ignorance.

> *Aham hi sarvagyanam bhokta ch*
> *prabhurev ch,*
> *Na tu mamabhijanantic*
> *tattevnatashachyavantic te.*

Because I am the Master and consumer of all *Yagyas*, people do not understand God in the name of *Yagya* as supreme *Tattva* and that is why their worship and *Yagya* do not result in complete fruiting. In summary, all these methods of worshipping through various names of God are directed towards one and the same supreme.

Now a question arises that when so many names and so many ways of worship relate to the same God; does this create any contradiction? Obviously, there is no contradiction at all. God is infinite and it is not possible for anyone to know Him completely. All scriptures and their commentary by learned ones (Rishis, munis, saints) have said Neti, Neti, Neti . . . . in describing the names and attributes of God.

When Sri Krishna showed His Universal form (in which the whole universe is manifested) to Arjuna, then, seeing the vastness of the form, a brave warrior like Arjuna got frightened. The vastness of God cannot be accommodated in our small brain. The entire universe is manifested in the grand frame of the body of God. We do not have the intellect in our mind and the power in our eyes to see and understand this Divine form of God. For the sake of convenience only, our Rishis have departmentalized the vastness into various *Dhams*, taking into account the attributes of God. But the fact is that God cannot be departmentalized in this manner. There is no boundary of those *Dhams*, nor any *Dhama* has been separated from each other by boundaries.

Avibhakt ch bhutesh vibhaktmiv ch
istitham,
Bhutbhartra ch tajaygyam grasishm ch.

Only one form of the God without departmentalization is present in all creatures separately. God, in the name of Vishnu holds and nurtures all creatures in this world. And in the name of Brahma gives birth to all.

Aditynamaham Vishnu jyortisham
raviranshuman
Marichimarutumism nakshtranamhame
shashi.

(In Suns I am Vishnu, in the light (radiance), I am seen, in airs I am *Marichi* air and in the planets I am moon).

Therefore, in the sky, the *Suryaloka, Chandraloka, Planetsloka and Vayuloka* all are parts of God. Although they appear to be separate, they are run in one thread and tell the vastness and omnipresence of all pervading everlasting *Tattva*, which stretches over in the entire Universe.

Let us go for a Pauranic story to further understand Vishnu.

Once upon a time a number of Rishis — Maharishis and Tapasvis assembled at the bank of river Saraswati. The point of discussion was, who is the most respected (the greatest) among Brahma, Vishnu and Shiv. To decide the issue Bhraguji was given the responsibility. Bhraguji met Brahma, Vishnu and Shiv separately.

Brahmaji expressed His annoyance, Shivji showed His anger and Vishnuji showed forgiveness. Bhraguji after testing the behavior of Brahma, Shiv and Vishnu, concluded, that the one who forgives even after being insulted is the greatest. Therefore, Lord Vishnu is the greatest. Bhraguji put forth his explanation as under:

Brahmaji performed the action of production (giving birth), where *Rajoguna* is dominant and due to his *Rajoguna* dominance Brahmaji was annoyed. Shivji with anger worked for dissolution; therefore there is the dominance of *Tamoguna*. And due to *Tamoguna* dominance Shivji became angry.

Lord Vishnu worked for preservation and nurtured this creation. That is why He showed forgiveness. Therefore, *Sattvaguna* was dominant in Him. In this manner Bhraguji, based on his testing, explained to Rishis — Maharishis that Lord Vishnu is the greatest.

> *Satyam sukha sanjayati ranjah karmni*
> *bharat,*
> *Gyanmavratya tu tamah pramade*
> *sanjaytyut.*

Hey, Arjuna! *Sattvaguna* engages in happiness, *Rajoguna* engages in action and *Tamoguna* camouflaging wisdom, engages in laziness and dullness.

SATELLITE CASTES *and* DEPENDENT RELATIONS